THE WALK SERIES

PRESSING ON TOWARD THE HEAVENLY CALLING

THE WALK SERIES

PRESSING ON
TOWARD THE
HEAVENLY CALLING

STEVE GALLAGHER

"Purity for Life"

www.purelifeministries.org

888.PURELIFE

Also available from Pure Life Ministries:

A Lamp Unto My Feet
At the Altar of Sexual Idolatry
At the Altar of Sexual Idolatry Workbook
A Biblical Guide to Counseling the Sexual Addict
Create In Me a Pure Heart
Entering His Courts
From Ashes to Beauty
He Leads Me Beside Still Waters
How America Lost Her Innocence
Intoxicated with Babylon
Irresistible to God
Living in Victory
Out of the Depths of Sexual Sin
Standing Firm Through the Great Apostasy
The Walk of Repentance
The Time of Your Life in Light of Eternity
Selah! The Book of Psalms in the Richest Translations

For these books and other teaching materials please contact:

Pure Life Ministries

14 School Street
Dry Ridge, KY 41035
(888) PURELIFE - to order
(859) 824-4444
www.purelifeministries.org

EAN 978-0-9758832-6-6
ISBN 0-9758832-6-7

"*Purity for Life*"
www.purelifeministries.org
888.PURELIFE

*I dedicate this book to every hungry soul
who will pound on Heaven's door until it opens,
cry out for mercy until their blind eyes see, and
wrestle with the Angel of the Lord
until they receive the blessing.*

Pressing On Toward the Heavenly Calling

CONTENTS

INTRODUCTION

The Prison Epistles are a divine archive of profound revelations about the kingdom of God, accumulated by a man who for many years enjoyed unbroken fellowship with the Lord. Each epistle possesses its own unique style and theme: Ephesians offers incredible glimpses into the heavenly domain inhabited by God and the powerful spiritual entities—both fallen and unfallen—who influence and affect mankind; Philippians is a joyful celebration of the vibrant Christian life; and Colossians focuses on the Christ, the great Center of the spiritual realm.*

Paul wrote these three books toward the end of his life. Having "fought the good fight… finished the course… kept the faith," he was now moving toward "the crown of righteousness, which the Lord, the righteous Judge" would award him. (II Timothy 4:6-8) For nearly thirty years, the "apostle to the Gentiles" had been *Pressing On Toward the Heavenly Calling.*

This twelve-week study of Ephesians, Philippians and Colossians can be extremely rewarding. However, it should be understood at the outset that such an examination can only be cursory at best. It is impossible for any single human to exhaust the riches of these three epistles—especially in 84 lessons. For instance, Dr. Martyn Lloyd-Jones wrote a commentary of six thick volumes solely on the book of Ephesians. I have studied his books and yet, when I read the writings of Joseph Beet, Albert Barnes, Alexander MacLaren and others, I find a wealth of new revelations never once touched upon by Lloyd-Jones!

Of course, it should go without saying that the student will derive precisely as much from this study as he desires. The casual reader will breeze through the lessons exerting little effort, content to impatiently answer questions without any real prayerful consideration. On the other hand, the earnest student will approach these treasure troves with anticipation and wonder. He will begin each day's homework with questions in his heart such as: "What

will I discover today?" and "How will God speak to my heart in this study?"

"Unless we realize our dependence upon the Holy Spirit the Word will not speak to us," penned Dr. Lloyd-Jones. "If we read the Word of God without praying for enlightenment, we shall probably get very little out of it. We must never depart from this consciousness of our dependence upon the Spirit's power and enlightenment. The 'anointing,' the 'unction from the Holy One,' of which the Apostle John speaks is needed constantly and increasingly."[1]

With that in mind, I would like to offer a few suggestions that I believe will help the reader maximize the benefits of this study through the Prison Epistles:

First, prayerfully approach each day's lessons. The Lord will speak to you and implant His wisdom in your heart if you will but ask Him. You do not need more biblical knowledge; you need a divine impartation! If you will ask, seek and knock, unexpected doors will be opened to you through Scripture. Approach the Word with expectancy and faith!

Second, be ever mindful that you live in a world that lies under a satanic enchantment. Spiritual darkness pervades our culture. The intoxicating voice of darkness blares at you relentlessly through television, radio and the Internet. It appears as truth, but is actually laced with underlying false messages, cunningly cloaked in seemingly innocuous information. The Bible is the one existing source of pure *truth*. Humble yourself before it and treat it with the utmost reverence.

Third, spend as much time as you can in your studies. You probably don't realize how much you have been polluted by the spirit of this world.† The more time you spend soaking in Scripture, the more you will take on the mind of God. Conversely, the more you immerse yourself in the world, the more its standards and values will shape your thinking and desires.

---

* The book of Philemon is also considered one of the "Prison Epistles," but due to space limitations will not be included in this study.

† For an exhaustive study on how the spirit of this world is affecting believers, please see my book, *Intoxicated with Babylon.*

Introduction - continued

If you feel as though you have already been terribly contaminated, don't despair! The Word of God can and will straighten out faulty perspectives, skewed attitudes and unlawful desires. You need only immerse yourself in it, allowing it to do its supernatural work inside you.

Last, please keep in mind that the Prison Epistles were written by a man with a great love for Scripture. To the spiritually dull, and those who are devoted to worldly entertainment, spending time in it will seem like a tedious, obligatory drudgery. To those who approach this study with a grateful, loving heart, it will become a "fountain of life."

You and I have embarked upon a lifelong spiritual journey. My hope is that this Bible study will help you as you continue *Pressing On Toward the Heavenly Calling.*

WEEK I: CHOSEN BY GOD

Monday

1. Read and meditate on Ephesians 1:1-14 (supplemental reading: Romans 1).

2. Depending upon the translation, Ephesians 1:3-6 is broken down into either one (KJV & NKJV), two (NASB), three (AMP & NIV) or even four (NLT) sentences. Carefully consider what this remarkable section of Scripture is saying. Using up to four sentences, rewrite this passage in your own words.

   a.

   b.

   c.

   d.

3. According to Ephesians 1:3, what have believers been blessed with?

4. According to Ephesians 1:4, for what purpose were believers chosen?

5. According to Ephesians 1:5, what were believers predestined to?

6. According to Ephesians 1:6, what was freely bestowed* upon believers?

7. Read the following verses and write out what it means to be *in Christ*.

   Ephesians 1:4

   Ephesians 1:7

   Ephesians 1:10b-11a

   Ephesians 1:13b

---

* The New American Standard Bible (which I use) translates the Greek phrase, "freely bestowed." However, it is rendered differently by other Bible translations, thus underscoring one of the unavoidable challenges of preparing this type of Bible study.

Tuesday

1. Read and meditate on Ephesians 1:1-14 (supplemental reading: Romans 2).

2. Again, depending upon the translation, Ephesians 1:7-12 is broken down into either one (KJV), two (NASB & NKJV) or three (AMP, NIV & NLT) sentences. Once again, ponder what is being expressed in this passage of Scripture. Using up to three sentences, rewrite it in your own words.

   a.

   b.

   c.

3. Compare the two statements made in Ephesians 1:6-8 about grace. Verse 6 says that it was "freely bestowed" (NASB & AMP), or "freely given" (NIV) to us.[†] Verse 8 states that it was "lavished" (NASB, NIV, & AMP) upon us. Look up the words *freely bestowed* (Gk. *charitoo*$_{5487}$)[‡] and *bestowed* (Gk. *perisseuo*$_{4052}$) in a Bible dictionary and list some of the synonyms provided for each.

   charitoo
   a.   b.

   c.   d.

   perisseuo
   a.   b.

   c.   d.

4. This second term, *perisseuo*, is especially interesting. Look up the following verses and tell what you learn about this word.

   Romans 15:13

   I Corinthians 15:58

   II Corinthians 1:5

   Philippians 1:9

---

† The King James Version expresses it differently.

‡ Throughout this study I have utilized the Strong's numbering system to aid the student with understanding Greek terms.

Wednesday

1. Read and meditate on Ephesians 1:1-14 (supplemental reading: Romans 3).

2. Rewrite Ephesians 1:13-14 in your own words.

3. Some people view the gospel almost as if it were nothing more than a lifeless tome of rules and regulations. By contrast, to the apostle Paul, the gospel was brimming with the life and Spirit of God. Look up Romans 1:16 and write out Paul's definition of the gospel.

4. Look up the following verses and describe what you learn about the Holy Spirit.

    Proverbs 1:23

    Luke 11:11-13

Wednesday - *continued*

John 7:38-39

John 16:13-15

Romans 8:5-6

I Corinthians 3:16

II Corinthians 3:17

Galatians 5:16-18

Galatians 5:22-23

Thursday

1. Read and meditate on Ephesians 1:15-23 (supplemental reading: Romans 4-5).

2. Why is Paul giving thanks in Ephesians 1:16?

3. According to Ephesians 1:17, what does Paul ask God to give to the readers of his epistle? Explain what you think he means by these terms.

4. In Ephesians 1:18-19a, Paul asks the Lord to enlighten the Ephesians so that they may know three things. List them.

    a.

    b.

    c.

5. It's obvious from Paul's writings that he considered it essential for a person's heart to be enlightened to spiritual truth. Look up the following verses (or phrase within a verse) and describe what you learn about the heart.

    Deuteronomy 5:28-29

    Psalm 51:17

Thursday - continued

Proverbs 4:23

Isaiah 29:13

Jeremiah 29:13

Joel 2:12-13

Matthew 6:21

Acts 5:3

Friday

1. Read and meditate on Ephesians 1:15-23 (supplemental reading: Romans 6-7).

2. What phrase in Philippians 3:10 best corresponds to what Paul is saying in Ephesians 1:19b-21? In what way are these verses a good commentary on Philippians 3:10?

3. According to Ephesians 1:20b-21, where is Christ seated?

4. According to Ephesians 2:6, where are believers seated?

5. Read the following verses in *The Amplified Bible* and write out what fresh insights or perspectives you gain from each.

   a. Even as [*in His love*] He chose us [*actually picked us out for Himself as His own*] in Christ before the foundation of the world, that we should be holy (consecrated and set apart for Him) and blameless in His sight, even above reproach, before Him in love. (Ephesians 1:4)

   b. For He foreordained us (destined us, planned in love for us) to be adopted (revealed) as His own children through Jesus Christ, in accordance with the purpose of His will [*because it pleased Him and was His kind intent*] (Ephesians 1:5)

   c. In Him you also who have heard the Word of Truth, the glad tidings (Gospel) of your salvation, and have believed in and adhered to and relied on Him, were stamped with the seal of the long-promised Holy Spirit. (Ephesians 1:13)

   d. That [*Spirit*] is the guarantee of our inheritance [*the firstfruits, the pledge and foretaste, the down payment on our heritage*], in anticipation of its full redemption and our acquiring [*complete*] possession of it—to the praise of His glory. (Ephesians 1:14)

Saturday

1. Read and meditate on Ephesians 1 (supplemental reading: Acts 6).

2. Review the sentences you wrote for question 2 in Monday and Tuesday's homework. Meditate upon the realities that have been expressed in Ephesians 1:3-12. It would be right to sit down and spend time thanking God for each one of these promises. Using the truths expressed in this passage, make a list of seven things for which you are grateful.

   a.

   b.

   c.

   d.

   e.

   f.

   g.

3. Review the verses about the Holy Spirit listed in question 4 of Wednesday's homework. Would you say that you have been filled with the Holy Spirit? According to Jesus, if we ask the Lord to fill us, He will. Prayerfully ponder each of these verses, asking God to fill you with His Spirit. Make this an ongoing prayer in the future.

Sunday

SAUL THE PHARISEE
Supplemental Reading: Acts 7:1-8:3
Time Frame: 2 B.C. - 36 A.D.

He was born in the great Cilician city of Tarsus, about the same time as that other Birth in Bethlehem. As a Pharisee and a Roman citizen, his father was undoubtedly one of the community leaders of their Jewish neighborhood. Young Saul grew up hearing the exploits of the heroes of the faith such as Abraham, Moses, David and the prophets. However, probably more impacting on his impressionable mind was watching his father's daily observances of the various religious rituals such as those surrounding the Sabbath. No doubt, the young lad watched with fascination as his father carefully donned his phylacteries and special shawl preparing for prayer.

Clearly, the adolescent determined to follow in his father's footsteps at an early age. He was probably no more than 13-years-old when his father announced that he had secured a highly coveted position for his son in the school of the great Jewish teacher Gamaliel in Jerusalem. One can only imagine the boy's excitement when he made the journey to the holy city he had heard about since earliest memory.

Soon, the gifted student was gathered with other excited boys around the famous doctor, listening attentively, asking questions and taking notes. Even in this elite group, Saul excelled. This constituted his life over the next twenty years: studying the oral law handed down by the Jewish rabbis, mastering the exacting work of the scribe and debating with his Saducean detractors. He was "a Hebrew of Hebrews; as to the Law, a Pharisee... as to the righteousness which is in the Law, found blameless." (Philippians 3:5-6) He later wrote, "I was advancing in Judaism beyond many of my contemporaries among my countrymen, being more extremely zealous for my ancestral traditions." (Galatians 1:14)

It is probable that Saul had returned to Tarsus before the wild-looking prophet named John came out of the Judean wilderness and began preaching repentance, baptizing people on the banks of the Jordan River. Thus, he would not have been present in Palestine during the 3½-year ministry of the Miracle-worker from detestable Galilee.§

By the time Saul returned to Jerusalem, his years of Pharisaical training had left him a miserably arrogant man, disdaining nearly everyone who came across his path. Had his heart been more receptive to Scripture, he would have learned that "a proud look" is an abomination to the Lord. (Proverbs 6:17) But Saul, well into his thirties by now, had become so self-righteous and self-absorbed that he saw no need for change in his life. Indeed, he would have gladly stood before the Lord God Himself—fully confident in *his own* righteousness.

This ugly spirit had permeated his inner being by the time a godly young man named Stephen— "full of grace and power" and "performing great wonders and signs among the people"—began preaching powerfully in Jerusalem. Luke tells us that "some from Cilicia and Asia, rose up and argued with Stephen." (Acts 6:9) Tarsus, we must remember, was the capital of Cilicia. Undoubtedly then, Saul, full of bitterness and pride, was one of those who tried to shout down the upstart Christian. When he and his friends found themselves "unable to cope with the wisdom and the Spirit with which he was speaking" (Acts 6:10), they dragged him to the closed chambers of the Jewish Sanhedrin. Saul and his friends produced false witnesses who accused him of speaking against the law and the temple.

When pressed about the charges, Stephen, seizing the opportunity, brilliantly recounted the history of the Jewish people's stubbornness. Then, suddenly, he passionately exclaimed, "You men who are stiff-necked and uncircumcised in heart and ears are always resisting the Holy Spirit; you are doing just as your fathers did. Which one of the prophets did your fathers not persecute? They killed those who had previously announced the coming of the Righteous One, whose betrayers and murderers you have now become; you who received the law as ordained by angels, and *yet* did not keep it." (Acts 7:51-54)

---

§ Had Paul actually seen or heard Jesus, which he surely would have had he been in Jerusalem during that time, he almost certainly would have mentioned it. Instead, he could only say that Jesus appeared to him later.

Sunday - continued

The piercing truth of his words "cut to the quick." They were so furious that "they *began* gnashing their teeth at him," and drove him out of the city where they stoned him to death. "Saul was in hearty agreement with putting him to death." (Acts 8:1a)

The martyrdom of Stephen appears to have opened the door to an all-out persecution of the fledgling Church. "Saul began ravaging the church, entering house after house, and dragging off men and women, he would put them in prison." (Acts 8:3) Luke's choice of wording here is very enlightening. *Ravaging* (Gk. *lumainomai*$_{3075}$) is the term used when describing wild beasts tearing and ripping at raw flesh.

It was as "a blasphemer and a persecutor and a violent aggressor" (I Timothy 1:13) that Saul went after the early Christians, locking "up many of the saints in prisons… also when they were being put to death I cast my vote against them. And as I punished them often in all the synagogues, I tried to force them to blaspheme." (Acts 26:10-11)

Raging like a madman, the pompous Pharisee did everything in his power to force believers to renounce Jesus as an imposter and deny that He was the Christ. Saul hated Him and everything the "would-be Messiah" represented. Finally, full of hatred and blood-lust, he went to the chief priest and begged permission to go to Damascus to hunt down more members of this despised sect. He had no idea what awaited him along that fateful road.

WEEK 2: ETERNAL EXHIBITION

Monday

1. Read and meditate on Ephesians 2:1-10 (supplemental reading: Romans 8).

2. Write out Ephesians 2:1-2.

3. In Ephesians 2:2, Paul dubs Satan, "the prince of the power of the air." Read the following passage from my book, *At the Altar of Sexual Idolatry*, and describe what you learn.

> The spirit of this world creates spiritual atmospheres conducive to lust…The world is full of lust. In practical terms, the spirit of this world capitalizes upon the fact that humans have carnal desires which are innate within them: the lust for pleasure, the lust for gain, and the lust for position. The enemy constantly attempts to create certain atmospheres which are tailor-made for the particular lust within us. Hence, the devil is called "the prince of the power of the air." For instance, if one were to go to a mall, he would find an atmosphere there which promotes covetousness. Women especially are vulnerable to the displays in the clothing stores. There is a spiritual climate there which provokes people to want more and more and more. Another example would be going to a boxing match. This environment incites pride, anger and ultimately, violence. These things can actually be felt "in the air." If one goes into a bar, the ambience puts him in a partying mood. Nevertheless, it is the enemy at work in each of these settings.[1]

4. In Ephesians 2:3, we find the phrase, "indulging the desires of the flesh and of the mind." Look up the word *desires* (Gk. *thelema*[2307]) in a Bible dictionary and describe what you learn.

5. "*Thelema*" is used four times in the first chapter (vv. 1, 5, 9, 11), where it is translated "will." How does this new information affect the way you understand Ephesians 2:3?

1. Read and meditate on Ephesians 2:1-10 (supplemental reading: Romans 9).

2. Write out Ephesians 2:4-5.

3. The apostle Paul uses the term "rich(es)" six times in the book of Ephesians. Look up each of the following verses and write out what this word is describing.

    a. Ephesians 1:7

    b. Ephesians 1:18

    c. Ephesians 2:4

    d. Ephesians 2:7

    e. Ephesians 3:8

    f. Ephesians 3:16

4. Read the following commentary by Dr. Martyn Lloyd-Jones and describe what you learn.

    What does 'to quicken' mean? It means 'to make alive,' it means 'to impart life'… Quickening is *regeneration*… Regeneration is an act of God by which a principle of new life is implanted in man, and the governing disposition of the soul is made holy. That is regeneration. It means that God by His mighty action puts a new disposition into my soul. Notice I say 'disposition,' not faculties. What a man in sin needs is not new faculties; what he needs is a new disposition. What is the difference, you ask between faculties and disposition? It is something like this: the disposition is that which determines the bent and the use of the faculties. The disposition is that which governs and organizes the use of the faculties, which makes one man a musician and another a poet and another something else. [*The Christian*] is not given a new brain, he is not given a new intelligence, or anything else. He has always had these; they are his servants, his instruments, his 'members' as Paul calls them in the sixth chapter of Romans; what is new is a new bent, a new disposition. He has turned in a different direction, there is a new power working in him and guiding his faculties.[2]

Wednesday

1. Read and meditate on Ephesians 2:1-10 (supplemental reading: Romans 10).

2. Rewrite Ephesians 2:6-7 in your own words.

3. Let us turn once again to the comments of Lloyd-Jones to better comprehend the incredible truth presented to us in Ephesians 2:7. After reading this, please describe what you have derived from it.

> The devil regards us with contempt, as he did Adam and Eve. He fawned upon them, he flattered them, because he knew that that was the way to make pawns of them. He had no interest in them at all as such. His own object was to detract from the glory and the majesty and the greatness of God. He was out to spoil God's work and God's world; he was out to ridicule it. He desired to stand up and to address all the holy angels and say: God makes claims for Himself, He says He has made a perfect world, but look at it, look at His perfect world! ...
>
> So God has initiated this great movement of redemption and of salvation primarily in order to declare and to manifest and to vindicate again His own glory, His own greatness and the truth about Himself....
>
> God has done all this, says Paul, in order that He may present a spectacle to all future ages, not only in this world but also in that which is to come. God is going to give a great demonstration, He is going to manifest His own glory....
>
> This is to me the most overwhelming thought that we can ever lay hold of, that the almighty, everlasting, eternal God is vindicating Himself and His holy nature and being, by something that He does in us and with us and through us....
>
> God is vindicating Himself and His character by you and by me, by people such as ourselves, by the whole of the Church gathered in Christ out of the world. He is going to put us on display, as it were; there is going to be a glorious exhibition. He is already doing it, but it is going to continue in the ages to come, and at the consummation God is going to open His last great exhibition and all these heavenly powers and principalities will be invited to attend. The curtain will draw back and God will say, Look at them![3]

4. Prayerfully read Revelation 14:1-5 and 15:1-4. Describe what you learn in light of what you have just read.

Thursday

1. Read and meditate on Ephesians 2:1-10 (supplemental reading: Romans 11).

2. God's grace, as revealed in the New Testament, can only be properly understood in the light of God's justice system in the Old Testament. If a Jew sinned in O.T. times, he had to face the full penalty of the law. When Jesus died on the cross, it did not mean that God quit hating sin and threw out His judicial system. It meant that the death of Jesus provided an atonement for the sin that had been committed. Rather than facing the due penalty of his sin, the perpetrator was now only expected to confess his sins and repent of them. In Ephesians 2:1-3, Paul urges the reader to consider that from which God has saved him. Can you see that a believer will never have a real revelation of grace until he comes to grips with the fact that he has been a criminal before God and deserves death? Explain your answer.

3. What would you say to the person who has the attitude that God's grace means that he can go on sinning willfully?

4. Do you think that a "monster" serial killer like Ted Bundy can be forgiven of his sins if he truly repents? Explain your answer.

5. God's grace also provides the power to break free from the power of sin. Look up the following passages of Scripture and describe what you learn about grace.

   II Corinthians 12:9

   Titus 2:11-14

6. According to Ephesians 2:10, what purpose did God have in your creation? Would you agree that this verse implies that He has prepared a special work in His kingdom just for you? Explain your answers.

Friday

1. Read and meditate on Ephesians 2:11-22 (supplemental reading: Romans 12).

2. Read Ephesians 2:19 and explain what you think Paul means by this statement.

3. According to Ephesians 2:19, with whom are *you* fellow citizens?

4. According to Ephesians 2:20, who is the foundation?

5. According to Ephesians 2:20, who is the cornerstone?

6. According to Ephesians 2:21 and 22, into what is this building growing?

7. Read Ephesians 2:3-7 in *The Amplified Bible* (provided below) and write out what fresh insights or perspectives you gain.

> Among these we as well as you once lived and conducted ourselves in the passions of our flesh [*our behavior governed by our corrupt and sensual nature*], obeying the impulses of the flesh and the thoughts of the mind [*our cravings dictated by our senses and our dark imaginings*]. We were then by nature children of [*God's*] wrath and heirs of [*His*] indignation, like the rest of mankind.
>
> But God—so rich is He in His mercy! Because of and in order to satisfy the great and wonderful and intense love with which He loved us, even when we were dead (slain) by [*our own*] shortcomings and trespasses, He made us alive together in fellowship and in union with Christ; [*He gave us the very life of Christ Himself, the same new life with which He quickened Him, for*] it is by grace (His favor and mercy which you did not deserve) that you are saved (delivered from judgment and made partakers of Christ's salvation).
>
> And He raised us up together with Him and made us sit down together [*giving us joint seating with Him*] in the heavenly sphere [*by virtue of our being*] in Christ Jesus (the Messiah, the Anointed One).
>
> He did this that He might clearly demonstrate through the ages to come the immeasurable (limitless, surpassing) riches of His free grace (His unmerited favor) in [*His*] kindness and goodness of heart toward us in Christ Jesus.

Saturday

1. Read and meditate on Ephesians 2 (supplemental reading: Galatians 1).

2. In Ephesians 2:4 we find one of the most marvelous couplings of any two words in Scripture: "But God…" The first three verses of Ephesians 2 were written to remind the reader what his life was like before he was rescued by Christ. I don't think it would be inappropriate to rephrase those verses something like this:

    *   Remember what it was like to be dead in your trespasses and sins,
    *   Remember what it was like to be devoted to this world system,
    *   Remember what it was like to be a follower of Satan,
    *   Remember what it was like to live in the lusts of the flesh,
    *   Remember what it was like to be utterly given over to carnality,
    *   Remember what it was like to have the wrath of God hanging over you.

    Believers tend to forget how empty, miserable and hopeless they once were. Use the statements above to ponder and then systematically explain what your life was like before coming to Christ.

3. Reread the passage about grace in question 2 of Thursday's homework. Do you feel that you have held a cheap view of God's grace? Read the following passage of Scripture from *The Amplified Bible* and explain what you learn and how it affects you.

    How much worse (sterner and heavier) punishment do you suppose he will be judged to deserve who has spurned and [*thus*] trampled underfoot the Son of God, and who has considered the covenant blood by which he was consecrated common and unhallowed, thus profaning it and insulting and outraging the [*Holy*] Spirit [*Who imparts*] grace (the unmerited favor and blessing of God)? (Hebrews 10:29)

Sunday

SAUL THE NEW CHRISTIAN
Supplemental Reading: Acts 9
Time Frame: 36 - 44 A.D.

The day Stephen died, something happened that forever changed the course of Saul's life. True, he was one of the leading protagonists responsible for having the Christian evangelist put to death. But one must wonder how it affected the young zealous Pharisee when Stephen's face shone "like the face of an angel" in the Council of the Sanhedrin. (Acts 6:15) What did Paul mean by this description that he later gave to Luke?*How did it affect him when the humble, dying evangelist exclaimed, "Behold, I see the heavens opened up and the Son of Man standing at the right hand of God?" We know that Saul and his friends "covered their ears and rushed at him with one impulse." (Acts 7:56-57) With his dying breath, Stephen uttered one, final prayer: "Lord, do not hold this sin against them!" God, in His mercy, honored that request.

Thus Saul, driven by hate but, at the same time, beckoned by a sovereign God, made the journey north toward Damascus. At midday, as they approached the Syrian capital, suddenly a light so bright that it paled the sun burst upon the small party of men. Some of his companions stood "speechless," while Saul was knocked to the ground. Then, out of that terror-inducing blaze of glory, came not the angry rebuke he would have expected from the hard taskmaster he served, but the sweetest, most loving voice he had ever heard. A simple question was posed to him: "Saul, Saul, why are you persecuting Me?"

Somehow, the stricken man pulled himself together enough to inquire who was speaking to him. "I am Jesus," came the reply. Those words must have exploded upon Saul's consciousness. "Jesus? *You* are the heretic from Galilee who deceived the people? You mean I have been wrong?!"

He had planned to strut into Damascus, the arrogant, triumphant persecutor. But now, he found himself led by the hand, a blinded and broken man, his remorse and shock so great that he could not eat or drink for three days. What must he have contemplated while lying in that bed for those 72 hours?

Undoubtedly, the first thing he considered was his 20 years of training as a Pharisee. Saul had devoted his entire life to learning the Scriptures and the oral traditions. His sense of self-worth was inextricably tied to the fact that he had been one of Gamaliel's star students. Now, he clearly saw his terrible error and the vain emptiness of it all.

Also, one unavoidable question must have plagued him: Why did he persecute those people? He could not escape the fact that the underlying reason was found in his arrogance and pride. Into his tortured mind flooded images of those hurt by his hatred: Stephen's child-like face as he asked God to forgive Saul and the others; the men he had had whipped and beaten—some even put to death; the women he had terrorized; and probably worst of all, those who he had successfully driven to renounce Christ under torture. "Why? Why? Why?"

He who had recited long prayers on street corners, who had prayed only to be seen by men, who had prayed thus to himself: "God, I thank You that I am not like other people: swindlers, unjust, adulterers, or even like this tax collector. I fast twice a week; I pay tithes of all that I get;" now was the one beating his breast saying, "God, be merciful to me the sinner!"

Intermingled with all of these painful memories must have also come the Old Testament passages, suddenly illuminated in a new light. Maybe he recounted Isaiah 53. "Oh!" it may have suddenly dawned on him, "the suffering Servant is Jesus whom I have been persecuting!" Unquestionably, such a revelation would have brought upon him another round of heart-wrenching repentance.

And yet, in the midst of all of this anguish, came tremendous hope and peace. The years of that stale, dead religion of countless rules and rituals were wiped away. In their place there was abundant life! The presence of God filled the room in which he lay. No doubt he thought of loved ones and friends who had also been deceived by Judaism. He must have been filled with excitement at the prospect of testifying to his brethren about what had happened. "Perhaps even Rabbi Gamaliel will open his heart to the Lord!"

---

* This information could have only been provided to Luke by an eyewitness—which must have been Paul.

Sunday - continued

After these three days of solitude, a humble man named Ananias arrived. God had appeared to him in a vision, telling him, "Go, for he is a chosen instrument of Mine, to bear My name before the Gentiles and kings and the sons of Israel; for I will show him how much he must suffer for My name's sake." (Acts 9:15-16) As Ananias laid hands upon the penitent man, scales fell from his eyes and he was filled with the Holy Spirit. Soon, other Christians arrived at the house and spent the next several days with him. Saul must have peppered them with a million questions.

Before long, the former persecutor of Christians was out on the streets preaching the message that Jesus truly was the long-awaited Messiah. After some time, he felt compelled to go into the wilderness of Arabia so that God could "reveal His Son in me." (Galatians 1:16) Three years later he returned to Jerusalem and spent two weeks with Peter and the other disciples.

He then journeyed to Tarsus, probably living there for only a year or so when he had another vision.† He later wrote, "I know a man in Christ who fourteen years ago… was caught up into Paradise and heard inexpressible words, which a man is not permitted to speak." (II Corinthians 12:2-4) Was it then that he saw the glory of the "heavenly bodies" believers would one day receive? (I Corinthians 15:40) Was this when he saw Christians seated "in the heavenly places in Christ Jesus?" (Ephesians 2:6) It is very well possible. One thing is certain, it all worked together to prepare him for the great calling that awaited him.

† The book of II Corinthians was written in 57 A.D., which tells us this experience occurred in the year 43, while he was still in Tarsus.

WEEK 3: EMPOWERED IN THE INNER MAN

Monday

1. Read and meditate on Ephesians 3:1-13 (supplemental reading: Romans 13).

2. According to Ephesians 3:3, how did Paul learn of the mystery about the Gentiles receiving the gospel?

3. According to Galatians 1:12, how did Paul learn about the gospel?

4. Try to imagine yourself living as a First-Century Jew. What would you have thought if a former Pharisee named Saul began asserting: 1) that the entire Jewish religion had gone astray, and 2) that he had a new revelation from the Lord about how a person should enter into a saving relationship with God?

5. Some people believe that the Lord no longer speaks to His people. A.W. Tozer, one of the godliest men of the past century, addressed this notion. Read his comments and describe what you learn.

    One [*fallacy*] is that God spoke the holy Scriptures into being and then elapsed into silence, a silence that will not be broken till God calls all men before Him to judgment. God will then speak again as in olden days, but in the meantime we have the Bible as a deposit of embalmed truth which scribe and theologian must decipher as they can....

    Now, the blessed fact is that God is not silent and has never been silent, but is speaking in His universe. The written Word is effective because, and only because, the Living Word is speaking in heaven and the Living Voice is sounding in the earth. "And it is the Spirit that beareth witness, because the Spirit is truth."...

    It is written that Christ upholds all things by the word of His power; and the word that upholds all things is the power-filled voice of God sounding vibrantly throughout the creation. The Bible is not, as some appear to think, God's last will and testament; it is, rather, the written expression of the mind of the Living God, inactive until the same breath that first inspired it breathes on it again.[1]

6. Look up Romans 8:14 and explain what you think Paul meant by this statement.

Tuesday

1. Read and meditate on Ephesians 3:14-21 (supplemental reading: Romans 14).

2. In your own words, rewrite Paul's wonderful prayer from Ephesians 3:16-19. Break your prayer down into distinct phrases.

   a.

   b.

   c.

   d.

   e.

   f.

   g.

   h.

   i.

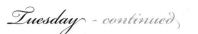*Tuesday - continued*

3. Read the following comments by Dr. Martyn Lloyd-Jones about Paul's prayer in Ephesians 3:16-19 and describe what you learn.

> Its intrinsic value demands attention at all times, but it is particularly relevant to the condition of the church today. Its experiential emphasis is needed urgently in view of certain alarming tendencies.
>
> One tendency is what is described as fideism or 'easy-believism.' This, in its crudest form, teaches that in light of Romans 10:9 if we but say that we believe, then we are saved. But still more dangerous, perhaps, is the highly intellectualist attitude which argues that in the light of [*Eph. 1:3*] all believers have already received everything possible to the Christian, and should never be seeking any further blessing. This erroneous teaching, which dislikes any emphasis on experience… [*leads*] to much spiritual dryness, hardness and barrenness….
>
> The common modern attitude which is so afraid of experiencing the love of God, because of the excesses of certain people who put experiences before truth, is virtually a defense of the attitude of the [*Laodiceans*] who said: "I have need of nothing."
>
> If I were asked to name the greatest trouble among Christians today, including those who are evangelical, I would say that it is our lack of spirituality and of a true knowledge of God….
>
> We can never know too much concerning the great doctrines of the Faith, but if that knowledge does not lead to an ever deeper experience of the love of Christ, it is merely the knowledge that "puffeth up."[2]

Wednesday

1. Read and meditate on Ephesians 3:14-21 (supplemental reading: Romans 15).

2. Paul's prayer, in Ephesians 3:16-19, describes a series of steps leading into the riches found in Christ alone. The beginning of the process is found in the phrase: "to be strengthened with power through His Spirit in the inner man." Read the following passage. Then, write out the eight statements in the second paragraph about what the power of God can do for the believer.

> There is a mighty force from heaven that is available to every child of God. The Lord greatly desires for you to be "clothed with power from on high." (Luke 24:49) He wants you to know about "the surpassing greatness of His power toward us who believe." (Ephesians 1:18-19) He wants it to be real to you that He "has not given us a spirit of timidity, but of power and love and discipline." (II Timothy 1:7) He longs for you to taste "the powers of the age to come," (Hebrews 6:5) and to experience "the power of an indestructible life." (Hebrews 7:16) He wants you to be "strengthened with all power, according to His glorious might… ." (Colossians 1:11) Yes, "The God of Israel Himself gives strength and power to the people. Blessed be God!" (Psalm 68:35)
>
> The great need for Christians today is for the invigorating life of God to flow through their beings, enlightening their minds with spiritual truth, purifying their motives, fortifying their convictions, molding their personalities, solidifying their vacillating wills, sweetening their natures, cleansing and renewing their hearts, and subduing their flesh. We need to be revitalized and energized by the quickening power of the Holy Spirit.
>
> Can God do this? My testimony is that I have seen it happen countless times in the most hopeless situations. Let the skeptics—both outside and within the Church—line up with their sneering cynicism and faithless denials of God's power. If they could but see within the walls of the celestial city, a hundred million saints would step forth with resounding testimonies to the fact that the Almighty converted them from virtual devils and made them loving saints.*

a.

b.

c.

d.

e.

f.

g.

h.

3. Ephesians 3:17b-19a contains a *conditional* promise. This means that God promises something but it is predicated upon some action of our own. Evaluate the following phrases. Explain how you think the condition expressed in the first phrase would allow a person to enjoy the promise of the second phrase.

Ephesians 3:17b: "that you, being rooted and grounded in love,"

Ephesians 3:18-19a: "may be able to comprehend with all the saints what is the breadth and length and height and depth, and to know the love of Christ which surpasses knowledge,"

---

* Steve Gallagher, unpublished material.

Thursday

1. Read and meditate on Ephesians 3:14-21 (supplemental reading: Acts 11).

2. Write out II Peter 1:4.

3. Compare Ephesians 3:19b with II Peter 1:4 and describe any similarities you find. Ponder the fabulous promises contained in these verses in the light of their context. Explain what you learn.

4. Now review what is expressed about Christ in Colossians 2:9. What new light does this shed on the statements found in Ephesians 3:19b coupled with II Peter 1:4?

5. Look up the following verses and, in one or two words, write what the person(s) is (are) filled with in each passage and/or situation. Afterward, explain what you learn about a human's capacity to be filled with a spirit or passion.

Matthew 23:27	Luke 1:15
Luke 4:28	Luke 5:26
Acts 2:4	Acts 3:10
Acts 5:17	Acts 6:8
Acts 13:52	Romans 1:29

Friday

1. Read and meditate on Ephesians 3:14-21 (supplemental reading: Acts 12).

2. Write out Ephesians 3:20.

3. The knowledge of God and the various aspects of His kingdom is not primarily obtained through mental exercise; it is something experienced in a person's heart. Look up the following two passages and describe what you learn.

   Matthew 11:25

   I Corinthians 2:12-14

4. Read Ephesians 3:16-20 in *The Amplified Bible* (provided below) and write out what fresh insights and/or perspectives you gain.

   May He grant you out of the rich treasury of His glory to be strengthened and reinforced with mighty power in the inner man by the [*Holy*] Spirit [*Himself indwelling your innermost being and personality*].
   May Christ through your faith [*actually*] dwell (settle down, abide, make His permanent home) in your hearts!
   May you be rooted deep in love and founded securely on love, That you may have the power and be strong to apprehend and grasp with all the saints [*God's devoted people, the experience of that love*] what is the breadth and length and height and depth [*of it*];
   [*That you may really come*] to know [*practically, through experience for yourselves*] the love of Christ, which far surpasses mere knowledge [*without experience*]; that you may be filled [*through all your being*] unto all the fullness of God [may have the richest measure of the divine Presence, and become a body wholly filled and flooded with God Himself]!
   Now to Him Who, by (in consequence of) the [*action of His*] power that is at work within us, is able to [*carry out His purpose and*] do superabundantly, far over and above all that we [*dare*] ask or think [*infinitely beyond our highest prayers, desires, thoughts, hopes, or dreams*]

Saturday

1. Read and meditate on Ephesians 3 (supplemental reading: Acts 13).

2. Review Tozer's remarks in Monday's homework (question 5). Do you ever sense the Holy Spirit convicting, leading or otherwise communicating to you? If not, does that raise concerns? Explain your answers.

3. Review Lloyd-Jones' comments in Tuesday's homework (question 3). How does your Christian life line up with what he is describing? Explain your answers.

4. Review question 3 in Wednesday's homework. It is simply an irrefutable law of the kingdom of God that the believer will only sense the love of Christ to the degree that he allows it to flow through his life into the lives of others. I once heard it illustrated using the action of the two seas in Palestine. The Sea of Galilee is brimming with life because the Jordan River flows into the northern end and flows out of the southern end. That flow does not allow the water to stagnate. On the other hand, although water flows into the Dead Sea, it never flows out again. Consequently, there is no life in it. So it is with Christians who continually want God's loving touch upon their lives but are unwilling to extend that love to other people. How will showing God's love to others help *you* to more fully comprehend the love of Christ? List at least 5 concrete ways you can do this.

Sunday

THE FIRST MISSIONARIES
Supplemental Reading: Acts 14
Time Frame: 44 - 48 A.D.

While Saul faced heartache and rejection from his family and friends in Tarsus, God was moving mightily among the Gentiles in Syrian Antioch. The revival was so powerful that it caught the attention of the disciples in Jerusalem. They sent Barnabas, one of the most trustworthy members of their congregation, to investigate. When he saw the magnitude of this move of God, he immediately left for Tarsus, knowing he needed the fire of Saul to help pastor this flock. For an entire year, the two men worked with the baby believers there in Antioch. Three other men joined them in their efforts: Simeon the black man; Lucius, who would later become a leader in the church at Corinth; and Manaen, foster brother of Herod Antipas.

When a prophetic word came forth that a great famine was imminent, the church sent Barnabas and Saul to Jerusalem with an offering. The two men arrived during the Passover, just in time to witness a fresh outbreak of persecution against Christians. James, one of the leading disciples, had been arrested and beheaded. Not long after this, Peter was also arrested and put in stocks in the main jail. As the big fisherman languished in his prison cell, the Church prayed fervently. Suddenly, an angel appeared to Peter and led him right out of the jail! He showed up at the home of Mary (John Mark's mother and the sister of Barnabas) surprising everyone there who had been praying—a group which probably included Barnabas and Saul.

Not long after this, an event occurred that is of particular significance because it establishes a firm date in the events recorded in the book of Acts. It is a well-documented fact that Herod Agrippa died of mysterious causes in the year 44 A.D. After this happened, Barnabas and Saul took Mark with them back to Antioch.

Several years passed as the church in Antioch continued to prosper under the spiritual leadership of the five pastors. One day, the leaders felt led to begin a special time of prayer and fasting for the Lord's direction. Of course, the last time Christian leaders had waited upon the Lord in this way, the great

Pentecostal outpouring was the result. Finally, one of the prophets received a direct word of knowledge: "Set apart for Me Barnabas and Saul for the work to which I have called them." (Acts 13:2)

What a thrill this must have been for Saul! Well over a decade had elapsed since he received the word from Ananias that he would bring the gospel to the Gentiles. Now it was finally going to happen! The other leaders prayerfully laid hands upon them and sent them out (along with Mark) as delegates to the heathen world. "So, being sent out by the Holy Spirit, they went down to Seleucia and from there they sailed to Cyprus," Luke later recorded. (Acts 13:4)

In the Cypriot capital of Paphos, they were afforded a tremendous opportunity when the Roman proconsul, Sergius Paulus, summoned them for a special meeting. At his side was a magician named Bar-Jesus. No doubt he had coined this name for himself some years before to capitalize upon the great works of the Jewish Wonder-worker. When this man opposed the missionaries, Saul, filled with the Holy Spirit, turned to him and said, "You who are full of all deceit and fraud, you son of the devil, you enemy of all righteousness… you will be blind and not see the sun for a time." (Acts 13:10-11) With that, he was instantly blinded. And it was here, at this time, that Saul finally shed his Jewish moniker and became Paul the apostle—taking for the first time the lead role in the venture.

The team left Cyprus and headed north by ship for Perga, a port city on the southern Asia Minor coast. Apparently, they had little success there and so prepared to make their way into the infamous Pamphylian hills that lie north of the city. This was a treacherous area, known for bands of robbers who preyed upon innocent travelers. Seemingly, this was too much for the young Mark who refused to continue, returning instead to Jerusalem.

Paul and Barnabas gratefully made it through without incident. It is quite possible that they intended to reach Ephesus and the other cities of the province of Asia. However, as they made their way through the Pamphylian hills, something happened to Paul's

Sunday - continued

eyes. Later, recounting the incident to the Galatians, he wrote: "but you know that it was because of a bodily illness that I preached the gospel to you the first time; and that which was a trial to you in my bodily condition you did not despise or loathe, but you received me as an angel of God, as Christ Jesus Himself. Where then is that sense of blessing you had? For I bear you witness that, if possible, you would have plucked out your eyes and given them to me." (Galatians 4:13-15)

And so, the two companions continued northward to the closer city of Pisidian Antioch. The very next Sabbath, Paul was allowed to share a message in the Jewish synagogue. As he preached, something powerful occurred and many people were touched by the Holy Spirit. By the following Saturday, the synagogue was packed with eager Anatolians. This was too much for the Jews, who were not about to have their synagogue overrun with filthy Gentiles! They raised a tumult, forcing Paul and Barnabas to flee the city.

The two men made the 90-mile walk to Iconium, where again many believed while others stood in staunch opposition. "They spent a long time there speaking boldly with reliance upon the Lord, who was testifying to the word of His grace, granting that signs and wonders be done by their hands." (Acts 14:3) When they discovered an assassination plot against them, they hurriedly left Iconium, heading for the small town of Lystra some 20 miles away.

One day, Paul happened by a paralyzed man, and saw, in some inexplicable way, that the man had faith to be healed. The apostle commanded him to stand and immediately the man leaped up and began to walk. This shocked the crowds, who hailed Paul as the Greek god Hermes, while calling Barnabas, Zeus. It was everything they could do to stop the people from worshiping them. Following on the heels of this incident, some Jews arrived from Antioch and incited the people to stone Paul. "But while the disciples stood around him, he got up and entered the city." This small group of Christians included a young man named Timothy.

The next day, Paul and Barnabas began the 60-mile trek to Derbe. After concluding their time there, it would have been a relatively short trip through the Cilician Gates and on back to their home in Syrian Antioch. But instead, they retraced their steps through the Galatian cities they had previously visited, "strengthening the souls of the disciples, encouraging them to continue in the faith, and saying, "Through many tribulations we must enter the kingdom of God." (Acts 14:22) They would learn soon enough the profound truth of this statement.

WEEK 4: HARDNESS OF HEART

Monday

1. Read and meditate on Ephesians 4:1-16 (supplemental reading: Romans 16).

2. Rewrite Ephesians 4:1-3 in your own words.

3. There are six distinct commands in these three verses. Ponder each of these and describe in detail what they mean to your life.

    a. "walk in a manner worthy of the calling with which you have been called,"

    b. "[live your life] with all humility,"

    c. "[live your life] with all gentleness,"

    d. "[live your life] with patience,"

Monday - continued

    e.   "showing tolerance for one another in love,"

    f.   "being diligent to preserve the unity of the Spirit in the bond of peace,"

4. In Ephesians 4:4-6, Paul provides reasons why Christians should be in unity. List the seven things he says that believers have in common.

    a.

    b.

    c.

    d.

    e.

    f.

    g.

Tuesday

1. Read and meditate on Ephesians 4:1-16 (supplemental reading: I Corinthians 1).

2. Read the following passage from the *Pulpit Commentary* and answer the questions that follow.

> The grand object of the apostle in this section of his Epistle is to show the ample provision made by Christ for the welfare of his Church. The Church may sing as well as the individual, "The Lord is my Shepherd; I shall not want."
>
> The particular object is to indicate that the gifts conferred by him on the members individually (vers. 7-11), and especially the appointment of the several classes of office-bearers (ver. 11), show the Lord's earnest desire to raise his Church to the highest possible condition of grace and honor; to make her complete and glorious, as the one body of which he is the Head, the one vessel into which he is to pour all his fullness, the bride on whom he is to exhaust every ornament.
>
> The marks of Christ's care for his Church are innumerable; they recede back through all eternity and forward for evermore (Ephesians 3:18, 19). His death marked the climax of his self-sacrifice; but even that did not end Christ's service for his Church. For her he not only descended from heaven to earth, but for her too he reascended from earth to heaven; like the high priest, he went into the holiest of all with his Name on his breastplate, and he only changed the sphere in which his mediatorial office was exercised.
>
> But more; the good Shepherd is ever renewing the miracle of the five loaves and two fishes; ever saying with reference to his people, "Give ye them to eat;" and ever appointing and qualifying suitable officers to take care of his Church and break among them the bread of life. He is ever qualifying his ministers for ruling and feeding his flock, for filling the empty soul, speaking a word in season to the weary, guiding the perplexed, reclaiming the erring, strengthening the weak, supporting the feeble-minded, and sending on the ransomed of the Lord to Zion, with songs and everlasting joy upon their heads.[1]

a. According to the first paragraph, what is Paul's "grand object?"

b. In the second paragraph, the commentator describes "the Lord's earnest desire." Rewrite this sentence in your own words.

c. According to the third paragraph, what are the two primary acts of service Christ has performed for His Church?

d. In the fourth paragraph, the commentator lists eight things his ministers are qualified to do. Summarize each of these duties using one or two words.

1. e.g.: Leading   2.

3.   4.

5.   6.

7.   8.

1. Read and meditate on Ephesians 4:17-32 (supplemental reading: I Corinthians 2).

2. In Ephesians 4:17-19, Paul employs the lives of unbelievers to supplement a negative commandment: "Do not live your life like they do." Examine each phrase of this passage and relate it to your own life. Describe what you think Paul is telling you not to allow in your life.

   a. "in the futility of their mind,"

   b. "being darkened in their understanding,"

   c. "excluded from the life of God because of the ignorance that is in them,"

   d. "excluded from the life of God because of the hardness of their heart,"

   e. "having become callous,"

   f. "have given themselves over to sensuality,"

Wednesday - *continued*

g. "for the practice of every kind of impurity with greediness."

3. Paul's phrase, "the hardness of their heart… having become callous," describes what happens to a person who gives over to sin. Elsewhere he spoke of those who were "seared in their own conscience as with a branding iron." (I Timothy 4:2) Read the following excerpt from an article I wrote and describe what you learn.

In the physical realm, the conscience is comparable to the human nervous system. When a person is wounded, he *feels* pain—the body's inherent means of alerting him that something is wrong. Likewise, when a person sins, the human soul has a warning system that sounds an alarm because the person's actions have *wounded him spiritually*. This soul-alarm trumpets, "Mayday! Mayday! Something is wrong!" He senses that his actions are not only wrong but will also result in destructive consequences.

A person with a tender conscience is keenly aware of every infraction against the Lord. He recognizes sin for the ugly thing that it is…. The person with a soft heart also remains consistently open to the Holy Spirit's conviction. He is not looking to push the limits of sin—to see how much he can get away with—but to avoid it altogether. Sin, to him, is a poison which must be eradicated at any cost.[2]

4. Explain in your own words what Paul meant in Ephesians 4:20.

Thursday

1. Read and meditate on Ephesians 4:17-32 (supplemental reading: I Corinthians 3).

2. Review Ephesians 4:22-32. List the ten things Paul instructs the believer to "put off," "lay aside" or avoid.

   a.   b.

   c.   d.

   e.   f.

   g.   h.

   i.   j.

3. Rewrite Ephesians 4:23-24 in your own words.

4. In Ephesians 4:23 Paul uses the Greek term *ananeoo*$_{365}$—the only time it is used in Scripture—which the NASB translates as *renew*. However, he employs its close cousins (Gk. *anakainoo*$_{341}$ and *anakainosis*$_{342}$) elsewhere. Look up the following verses and describe what you learn in each verse.

   Romans 12:2

   II Corinthians 4:16

   Colossians 3:10

   Titus 3:5

5. According to Ephesians 4:32, what three things are believers supposed to do?

   a.

   b.

   c.

Friday

1. Read and meditate on Ephesians 5:1-21 (supplemental reading: I Corinthians 4).

2. Paul opens Ephesians 5 with a continuation of commandments about the way believers ought to live their lives. For each verse listed below, write a *P* next to it if it is a positive command (i.e. "Do this.") and an *N* if it is a negative command (i.e. "Do not do this.").

Ephesians 5:1a- e.g. *P*   Ephesians 5:2a

Ephesians 5:3a- e.g. *N*   Ephesians 5:4a

Ephesians 5:7   Ephesians 5:11a

Ephesians 5:15a   Ephesians 5:16

Ephesians 5:17a   Ephesians 5:17b

Ephesians 5:18a   Ephesians 5:18b

Ephesians 5:19a   Ephesians 5:19b

Ephesians 5:20   Ephesians 5:21

3. To what do you think Paul is referring in Ephesians 5:6 when he warns the reader not to allow himself to be deceived?

4. Look up the other similar warnings found in the following passages and describe what you think is being stated by the writer.

I Corinthians 6:9-10

Friday - continued

I Corinthians 15:33

Galatians 6:7-8a

James 1:14-16

5. Look up each of the following terms in a Bible dictionary and describe what you learn.

    a. *immoral* (Gk. *pornos*$_{4205}$)

    b. *impure* (Gk. *akathartos*$_{169}$)

    c. *covetous* (Gk. *pleonektes*$_{4123}$)

Saturday

1. Read and meditate on Ephesians 4:1-5:21 (supplemental reading: Galatians 2).

2. Review the commandments listed in question 2 of yesterday's homework and prayerfully evaluate your obedience to each command (you may wish to grade yourself as A, B, C, D, or F on each).

   a.   b.

   c.   d.

   e.   f.

   g.   h.

   i.   j.

   k.   l.

   m.   n.

   o.   p.

3. Now choose 4 or 5 areas you could improve on personally, describing in detail what changes you will make to "put off" the ungodly behavior or "put on" the appropriate behavior.

   a.

   b.

   c.

   d.

   e.

SAVED BY GRACE
Supplemental Reading: Acts 15
Time Frame: 48 - 51 A.D.

The religious difficulty in the mind of a First-Century Jew toward Gentile Christianity was greater than we, in this present age of obligatory tolerance, can easily imagine. For generations, Jews had been strictly taught that it was part of their heritage and faith to separate themselves from Gentiles.

Of course, it was always possible for Gentiles to convert and become Jewish proselytes. However, this was a monumental event accomplished through a grueling series of Judaic rituals aimed at nothing less than the complete overhauling of a person's identity. It began with the rite of circumcision and the complete renunciation of everything considered unclean to the Jewish mind. A proselyte was expected to walk away from all unconverted friends and family members and become an utterly new person.

From Christianity's inception, it was viewed rightly by the Jewish believer to be the fulfillment of the Jewish Scriptures. Indeed, devout Jews considered it the answer to all their hopes and aspirations as a people. Even Jesus had made statements like: "I was sent only to the lost sheep of the house of Israel" and "It is not good to take the children's bread and throw it to the dogs." (Matthew 15:24, 26)

So, when Gentiles began their wholesale acceptance of the Jewish Messiah as their Savior also, it only stood to reason that this meant that they were becoming, in effect, Jewish proselytes. Understandably then, it was assumed that they would naturally undergo the ritualistic changeover process—beginning with circumcision.

But nobody could have anticipated what transpired in Antioch—a Roman city a couple hundred miles north in Syria. Christianity there was spreading like wildfire amongst the heathen population.

After Peter's experience with Cornelius, most Jewish believers were coming to grips with the rapidly unfolding reality: God was birthing an entirely new religion that would bypass the Judaic legal system and rest entirely on the union of man's faith and God's grace. Unfortunately, within the ranks of the young Church was a group who stubbornly refused to accept God's plan. They became known as "Judaisers," or "the party of the circumcision." As Pharisees, they could believe that Jesus was resurrected from the dead and even assent to Him being the Messiah. What they simply could not accept—in their Jewish pride—was a salvation that was free for one and all. To them, it reeked of cheap grace and easy believe-ism.

It must be remembered that, in the Jewish mind, Gentiles were considered "dogs." Not only were they less civilized in the sense of cleanliness and eating habits, but they were also wantonly given over to the worst kinds of licentious behavior. In fact, their temples were little more than brothels, with rampant homosexuality and prostitution as the centerpieces of their worship. The thought of opening the doors of the Church to such filthy people was unthinkable.

Jerusalem was the metropolis of the Jewish world. The exclusive feelings which the Jews carried with them wherever they were diffused, were concentrated in Jerusalem in their most intense degree. It was there, in the sight of the Temple, and with all the recollections of their ancestors surrounding their daily life, that the impatience of the Jewish Christians kindled into burning indignation. They saw that Christianity, instead of being the purest and holiest form of Judaism, was rapidly becoming a universal and indiscriminating religion, in which the Jewish element would be absorbed and lost. This revolution could not appear to them in any other light than as a rebellion against all they had been taught to hold inviolably sacred. And since there was no doubt that the great instigator of this change of opinion was that Saul of Tarsus whom they had once known as a young Pharisee at the "feet of Gamaliel,"'the contest took the form of an attack made by "certain of the sect of the Pharisees" upon St. Paul. The battle which had been fought and lost in the 'Cilician synagogue' was now to be renewed within the Church itself.[3]

Sunday - continued

This great controversy brewing within the Church occasioned the summoning of Paul and Barnabas to Jerusalem. At this point, we find the Church in the midst of a transition of leadership. Following Pentecost, Peter and the other ten disciples were the undisputed spiritual leaders of this vibrant, new religion. Now, some 17 years later, we find James, the brother of Jesus, as the leader of the "elders," and holding joint leadership of the Church with the disciples. Later, the disciples—the eye-witnesses of the resurrection of Christ—were sent out across the known world with their message while the church in Jerusalem became solely governed by the elders.

Paul and Barnabas arrived at the meeting of the Council, sharing their experiences in Galatia. After a great deal of debate, Peter stood up and reminded everyone of what God had shown them through his experience with Cornelius, some 14 years before. Finally, James issued his verdict. The Council would issue a letter to the Gentile Christians acknowledging that it was by grace that they were saved, that they would not be expected to keep the Jewish law However, it did ask them to abide by three requirements: 1) To abstain from eating food offered to idols, something the Jews considered to be reprehensible; 2) To abstain from any kind of immorality; and, 3) To abstain from eating the meat of animals that had been strangled and thus still held its blood. This was a shrewd compromise intended to maintain the truth of Paul's message (saved by grace and not by works) and yet also to appease Jewish sensitivity to decency. This letter was sent to the Antiochian believers by two of the elders of the Jerusalem church, Judas and Silas.

Paul and Barnabas returned to Antioch triumphantly, remaining there for a period of several months, during which Peter paid a visit to the church. What a tremendous blessing it must have been to the believers there to actually hear the great disciple preach in their midst! Peter openly fellowshipped with these Gentiles; that is, until a band of Judaisers showed up from Jerusalem. Then, he suddenly distanced himself from his new brothers. Paul could not stand for this blatant hypocrisy and confronted him in front of everyone! "If you, being a Jew, live like the Gentiles and not like the Jews, how *is it that* you compel the Gentiles to live like Jews?" (Galatians 2:14) In other words, "You are demanding that the Gentile believers adhere to rituals which you yourself have renounced!" Poor Peter. All these years after the death of Jesus and once again he finds himself being publicly rebuked. And yet it was right, because the big fisherman's fear of man had led him to align himself with the early Church's worst heresy. Peter repented and the doctrinal dispute was resolved, but this was a battle Paul would face again.

WEEK 5: THE REALM OF CAUSE

Monday

1. Read and meditate on Ephesians 5:22-6:9 (supplemental reading: I Corinthians 5).

2. Ephesians 5:22-33 is the most complete instructional treatise on marriage in the entire Bible. In this passage of Scripture, there is one basic command given to the husband and one to the wife. Write out these two commands.

   a. Husbands:

   b. Wives:

3. Write out what Christ calls "the second great commandment" found in Matthew 22:39.

4. Some people teach that this great commandment means a person cannot love others until he first loves himself; therefore, he must focus on building his own self-esteem. But in Ephesians 5:28-29, Paul makes the point that people already love themselves—so much so that he compares it to Christ's love for the Church. The problem is not a lack of love for oneself but an overabundance of it! Read the following verses. Then, in the space provided below, discuss what the Bible teaches on this subject.

   Philippians 2:3-4

   II Timothy 3:1-2a

Monday - continued

5. Describe what it would really be like if a Christian home lived by the standards provided in Ephesians 6:1-4.

6. Ephesians 6:5-9 deals with the relationship between masters and slaves. In our culture, this analogy translates into the modern workplace. Ephesians 6:5-8 offers several characteristics that exemplify an employee's obedient attitude toward his boss. List three of these and provide your own explanation of each.

   a.

   b.

   c.

Tuesday

1. Read and meditate on Ephesians 6:10-24 (supplemental reading: I Corinthians 6).

2. Write out Ephesians 6:10.

3. In recent times, Ephesians 6:10-17 has become the focus of various misguided teachers. They have made the classic mistake of superficially focusing on the outward illustration rather than on the real, underlying meaning of the passage. I don't think Paul ever imagined that one day readers of this epistle would actually dress up in Roman costumes to re-enact what he was expressing. Paul used the analogy of a soldier's armor simply to show how the believer's daily life with God is what provides the needed protection to live in a devil-infested world. With that in mind, ponder each element of the believer's armor and describe its importance as a defense against the enemy's attacks in your daily life.

   a. Truth

   b. Righteousness

   c. The preparation of the gospel of peace

   d. Faith

Tuesday - continued

   e. Salvation

   f. The Word of God

   g. Prayer

4. Prayer is one of the key elements to a vibrant life in God. Read the following commentary and describe what you learn about its importance.

> To the Christian soldier, however, it is indispensable. Prayer crowns all lawful efforts with success and gives a victory when nothing else would. No matter how complete the armor; no matter how skilled we may be in the science of war; no matter how courageous we may be, we may be certain that without prayer we shall be defeated. God alone can give the victory; and when the Christian soldier goes forth armed completely for the spiritual conflict, if he looks to God by prayer, he may be sure of a triumph. This prayer is not to be intermitted. It is to be always. In every temptation and spiritual conflict we are to pray…. With all kinds of prayer; prayer in the closet, the family, the social meeting, the great assembly; prayer at the usual hours, prayer when we are specially tempted, and when we feel just like praying, prayer in the form of supplication for ourselves, and in the form of intercession for others. This is, after all, the great weapon of our spiritual armor, and by this we may hope to prevail.[1]

Wednesday

1. Read and meditate on Ephesians 6:10-24 (supplemental reading: I Corinthians 7).

2. Rewrite Ephesians 6:12 in your own words.

3. Look up each of the following terms in a Bible dictionary and describe what you learn about each.

    a.   rulers (Gk. *arche*₇₄₆)

    b.   powers (Gk. *exousia*₁₈₄₉)

    c.   world forces (Gk. *kosmokrator*₂₈₈₈)

    d.   darkness (Gk. *skotos*₄₆₅₅)

    e.   wickedness (Gk. *poneria*₄₁₈₉)

4. Read the following passage from my book *Living In Victory* and explain what you learn about spiritual warfare.

    Spiritual warfare has become quite a sensation in the American Church. Prayer groups meet in our churches where part of the corporate prayer time is spent "pulling down strongholds." Macho saints at spiritual warfare conferences go around karate chopping imaginary demons. Believers in deliverance churches sometimes writhe on the floor, screaming, and retching as others "cast demons out of them." Groups go out to the red-light districts and march around bars and porn shops "taking authority" over the ruling devils there. Others spend the bulk of their prayer times talking to demons, roaring like lions, binding and loosing, renouncing and breaking generational curses....

    Do I believe in deliverance? Absolutely! Jesus set people free from evil spirits. Paul cast demons out of people. We can do it today, too, but first we must have an infilling of the Spirit that gives us that kind of authority over those devils. However, it should be noted that these two (Jesus and Paul) didn't hold special deliverance services or spiritual warfare conferences. Totally surrendered to God's will, they simply went about doing deeds of mercy, which sometimes included casting devils out of those oppressed.

    Unfortunately, many believers want the power without the sacrifice. They want to feel like mighty men or women of God who can command the devils of hell to obey them. They are more interested in how it makes them look or feel than in the well-being of those in need. They imagine themselves in a place of authority that simply doesn't exist. They think that the name of Jesus gives them carte blanche in the spirit realm and devils have to obey their every word. But it doesn't work that way....

    The believer who lives in the words of Jesus, such as those given in the Sermon on the Mount, will have the power of God in his life and will hold authority over every devil he encounters. *The victory he wins over his own rebellious nature allows him to be victorious over the enemy....* Show me one believer who quietly lives the love of God and I will show you someone that leaves the devils of hell shaking. This precious saint will never hear, "I recognize Jesus, and I know about Paul, but who are you?"[2]

Thursday

1. Read and meditate on Ephesians 6:10-24 (supplemental reading: I Corinthians 8).

2. According to Ephesians 6:12, where are "the spiritual forces of wickedness?"

3. Look up the word *heavenly* (Gk. *epouranios*$_{2032}$) in a Bible dictionary and describe what you learn.

4. The word *heavenly* can refer to God's home or to the atmosphere of earth inhabited by spiritual beings. In either case, this word describes the *realm of cause* in contrast to the *world of effects*. In other words, the things that take place on earth are very often a direct result of influences from or actions taken in the spiritual realm. Look up the following verses and describe what you learn about this word

   John 3:12

   Ephesians 1:3

   Ephesians 3:10

   Philippians 2:10

5. According to Scripture, Satan has or will experience three great falls. His first fall was when he was cast out of heaven (God's dwelling place) into the earth's atmosphere. The devil's second fall is when he will be cast out of the atmosphere (heavenly places) onto the earth. The third occurrence will be when he is cast into the lake of fire. Look up the following verses and write a "1," "2" or "3" to designate which fall is being referenced.

   Revelation 12:9   Luke 10:18

   Revelation 20:10   Isaiah 14:12a

Friday

1. Read and meditate on Ephesians 6:10-24 (supplemental reading: I Corinthians 9).

2. Write out Ephesians 6:11.

3. According to Ephesians 6:11, what is the objective of putting on the armor of God?

4. According to Ephesians 6:13, what is the objective of putting on the armor of God?

5. Explain the correlation between these two verses as you see it.

6. Read Ephesians 6:10-14 in *The Amplified Bible* (provided below) and write out what fresh insights or perspectives you gain.

> In conclusion, be strong in the Lord [*be empowered through your union with Him*]; draw your strength from Him [*that strength which His boundless might provides*].
> Put on God's whole armor [*the armor of a heavy-armed soldier which God supplies*], that you may be able successfully to stand up against [*all*] the strategies and the deceits of the devil.
> For we are not wrestling with flesh and blood [*contending only with physical opponents*], but against the despotisms, against the powers, against [*the master spirits who are*] the world rulers of this present darkness, against the spirit forces of wickedness in the heavenly (supernatural) sphere.
> Therefore put on God's complete armor, that you may be able to resist and stand your ground on the evil day [*of danger*], and, having done all [*the crisis demands*], to stand [*firmly in your place*].
> Stand therefore [*hold your ground*], having tightened the belt of truth around your loins and having put on the breastplate of integrity and of moral rectitude and right standing with God.

Saturday

1. Read and meditate on Ephesians 5:22-6:24 (supplemental reading: I Corinthians 10).

2. Review the three primary relationships discussed in Ephesians 5:22-6:9. Examine your own life regarding your close relations. Without taking into account how others treat you, describe how well you live up to what is expressed by Paul. (Singles should skip the first).

   a. Husbands and wives:

   b. Parents and children:

   c. Employers and employees:

3. Review the passage found in question 4 of Wednesday's homework. The point of this text is that a believer's authority directly relates to the degree he is submitted to and controlled by the Holy Spirit. The truly godly life will be manifested through the person's loving involvement in the lives of others. How concerned are you with helping others? Have you yet found your niche in the kingdom of God? Are you occupied with meeting the needs of others? Can you see how living out the love of God to others would increase your spiritual authority? Explain your answers.

4. Review questions 3 and 4 in yesterday's homework. Can you see how having a strong relationship with God would prepare you to withstand the (sometimes) powerful temptations the enemy can bring your way? When was the last time you were really tempted to sin? What was the outcome of it? Did you feel God's power available to you to help you withstand it? Explain your answers.

REJOICE IN SUFFERING
Supplemental Reading: Acts 16
Time Frame: 51 - 52 A.D.

Paul could once again feel a sense of burden mounting in his heart. The time had come to venture out of the safe and comfortable confines of Syrian Antioch, back into the unpredictable life of the missionary. As Paul and Barnabas discussed their next journey, the name of John Mark surfaced. Barnabas wanted to give his nephew the opportunity to redeem himself after his earlier failure. Paul vehemently disagreed, feeling that Mark was not trustworthy. He was also concerned about how it would affect the people they were attempting to reach if one of their party suddenly abandoned them. Perhaps he even quoted the words of Jesus: "No one, after putting his hand to the plow and looking back, is fit for the kingdom of God." (Luke 9:62) Barnabas, on the other hand, felt that Mark had matured during the four years since the first trip and deserved another chance.

The disagreement highlights the two types of leaders at work in Christianity. There are visionaries, like Paul, who see the big picture and what is best for everyone involved. Then there are "sons of encouragement," who focus on the needs of the individual. When the Church keeps the proper balance, the strengths of both can be utilized. Unfortunately, in this case, the disagreement turned into a heated argument. Nevertheless, God brought good out of the situation as two evangelistic teams now left Antioch: Barnabas and Mark to Cyprus and Paul with Silas to Galatia.

On this trip, Paul chose to travel northwest by land, through the Cilician Gates, and on to the cities of Galatia. The presence of an elder of the church of Jerusalem with him surely made a positive impression on these believers who had become poisoned by the Judaisers. Silas was able to share with them the letter written from the Council which undoubtedly helped allay their concerns.

While in Lystra, Paul recruited a young man who would prove to be an invaluable disciple for many years to come. Only four years before, Timothy had witnessed the apostle being stoned by his fellow townspeople. Since that time, he had developed a reputation of faithfulness among Christian leaders in both Lystra and Iconium. Paul circumcised the half-Jewish young man and held a special ordination service for him. During this meeting, as Paul and the local leaders laid hands upon him, he received a "gift of God," (II Timothy 1:6) "through prophetic utterance." (I Timothy 4:14)

Paul, Silas and Timothy soon left Iconium, briefly visited Cilician Antioch, then departed the Galatian region, heading northwest toward Bithynia. But the Holy Spirit would not allow them to go into this region, instead directing them to Troas. While at this Aegean seaport, Paul had a vision where he apparently was allowed to see the cry of someone's heart in Macedonia.

The next day, along with a recently converted physician named Luke, they traveled by boat to Neapolis, where Paul's feet touched European soil for the first time. The small band of companions walked along the famous Ignatian Way until they reached the Roman colony of Philippi, some 30 miles away. Doubtless, they interceded fervently for souls to be saved as they neared the city. Those entreaties would be answered in an entirely unforeseeable way.

Philippi had no synagogue in which to preach, but the company heard that a group of Jewish women regularly met by the river to worship. Paul attended one of their meetings and shared the gospel with them. "The Lord opened the heart" of a businesswoman named Lydia, who invited them to stay in her home.

Over the ensuing days, a demon-possessed girl began following them around loudly proclaiming, "These men are bond-servants of the Most High God, who are proclaiming to you the way of salvation." (Acts 16:17) One might wonder why this would bother Paul. After all, he was in a heathen city where no one knew the Lord. This girl, paid to give "wisdom" to people, was affirming that they were telling the truth.

However, it is important to understand that the Philippians were polytheistic. To them, Paul was simply proclaiming one more of a host of pagan gods.

Besides that, Paul did not want the pure word of the gospel contaminated by being attached in people's minds to a fortune teller.

Nonetheless, Paul eventually grew annoyed over her rantings and cast the demon out of her. The change in her must have been dramatic. Suddenly, she was in her "right mind." When her masters saw that she had lost her clairvoyant powers, they became furious and grabbed Paul and Silas, forcibly dragging them to the city magistrates. "These men are throwing our city into confusion, being Jews, and are proclaiming customs which it is not lawful for us to accept or to observe, being Romans," they yelled. (Acts 16:20-21)

In the Roman Empire, Jews were universally disliked and mistrusted, which was all the proof the officials needed that Paul and Silas were troublemakers. Without even allowing them to offer a defense, they ordered them beaten with rods. Once the pummeling was completed, they were hauled off to the innermost part of the jail and secured in stocks. The jail in Philippi was nothing more than a cave in the side of a mountain, the innermost cell simply its deepest hole. The stocks they were put in were created as instruments of torture, mercilessly spreading the arms and legs of the person to the point where one could find no comfort or rest.

As the men stood stretched apart, racked with pain, time seemingly must have come to a standstill. Nevertheless, hours later we find them praying and rejoicing in the Lord. (Acts 16:25) Of course, mature believers understand that the best way to escape physical discomfort is to throw oneself into the spiritual realm of God. It is very likely that they were singing through one of the Psalms when a mighty earthquake shook the mountain housing the jail. The jailer, assuming all the prisoners had escaped, was ready to take his own life; but Paul stopped him. The man came trembling to the beaten apostle asking how he might find this God to whom they prayed.

And thus, the Philippian church was birthed with a handful of Jewish ladies, a girl who had been possessed by a devil and the jailer and his family. These fledgling saints would prove to be among Paul's staunchest friends in the years to come.

WEEK 6: SAINTS OF GOD

Monday

1. Read and meditate on Philippians 1:1-11 (supplemental reading: I Corinthians 11).

2. According to Philippians 1:1, to whom was this epistle written?

3. Look up the word *saints* (Gk. *hagios*$_{40}$) in a Bible dictionary and list some of the synonyms provided.

    a.   b.

    c.   d.

4. Read the following passage from *Intoxicated with Babylon*. Carefully consider what is being expressed here and then give a thorough explanation about what you learn of this Greek term.

> Having been delivered "from the domain of darkness, and transferred to the kingdom of His beloved Son", (Colossians 1:13) they would live separated from this world's system, set apart as consecrated vessels for God's use. They would be known as saints, (Greek *hagios*, "separated ones, set apart ones, holy ones")....
>
> The corporate body of these "separated ones" is called the church (Greek *ekklesia*, from *ek*, which means *out of*, and *kletos*, which means *called*). In Old Testament language, God's called out ones were "the congregation of the Lord;" in the New Testament they are "the church," the "called out ones."....
>
> Listen to the explanation of the meaning of such words from the pen of W. B. Godbey, a fiery preacher of the 19th Century.
>
> *Ekklesia*, from *ek*, out, and *kaleo*, to call, means Church throughout the Greek New Testament. If you do not remember that definition you will fall into utter bewilderment on the Church idea, led astray by the Churchism of the present day, which is utterly variant from, and antagonistical to the New Testament *ekklesia*, which consisted only of the souls called out of the world, and separated unto God. Hence, all worldly churches are simply Satan's counterfeits....
>
> This is the glorified Church of the First Born, "without spot or wrinkle." The members of this Church are not joined in, but born into it, by the supernatural intervention of the Holy Ghost. This is none of your worldly Churches, as the very word for Church, *ekklesia*, means *the called out of the world*; while *hagiadzoo*, sanctify, means *to take the world out of you*.
>
> Hence, all the members of the New Testament Church have a double reason for being unworldly; the one because they have come out of the world, and left it; and the other, because the world has been taken out of them. Hence, there is a double divorcement between them and the world. (emphasis added)[1]

Tuesday

1. Read and meditate on Philippians 1:1-11 (supplemental reading: I Corinthians 12).

2. Write out Philippians 1:6.

3. Why do you think Paul could make this confident statement regarding the Philippian believers?

4. Read Psalm 138:7-8. Write out the four statements David makes expressing what he is confident the Lord will do for him.

    a.

    b.

    c.

    d.

5. In Philippians 1:7-8, Paul expresses his feelings toward the believers of Philippi. According to verse 7, why is it "only right" for him to feel this way about them?

6. How does he express these feelings in verse 8?

7. In your own words, summarize Paul's prayer in Philippians 1:9-11.

Wednesday

1. Read and meditate on Philippians 1:12-20 (supplemental reading: I Corinthians 13).

2. According to Philippians 1:15-17, some were preaching Christ out of love, but others had a different motive. Describe, in your own words, the motive and purpose of these *others* who were preaching Christ.

3. A. W. Tozer wrote, "The churches are cluttered with religious amateurs culturally unfit to minister at the altar, and the people suffer as a consequence.... Much that is being done in Christ's name is false to Christ in that it is conceived by the flesh, incorporates fleshly methods, and seeks fleshly ends."[2] Look up the following verses and explain what you learn about false or unqualified teachers.

    Matthew 7:15-20

    II Corinthians 2:17

    II Corinthians 10:12

    II Corinthians 11:13-15

    Philippians 3:18-19

    I Timothy 1:6-7

    II Peter 2:1-3

    II Peter 2:17-19

    I John 4:5

    Jude 1:4

Thursday

1. Read and meditate on Philippians 1:21-30 (supplemental reading: I Corinthians 14).

2. Rewrite Philippians 1:21 in your own words.

3. Paul's statement in Philippians 1:21 must have been extremely precious to the Lord. It is an expression of the highest devotion one can have toward God. "To live is Christ…" A deep life in God backed up those words—words that have been thrown around cheaply by others over the years. The Greek word for live is *zao*, which is the verb form of the noun *zoe*. Read the following passage from *Intoxicated With Babylon* and explain what you learn in light of Philippians 1:21.

> On another occasion, Jesus slightly altered the second statement: "He who loves his life (Greek, *psyche*) loses it; and he who hates his life (*psyche*) in this world (*kosmos*) shall keep it to life (*zoe*) eternal." (John 12:25) The deliberate choice of words for "life" sheds light on the real meaning. *Psyche* represents one's existence on earth, while *zoe* represents one's life in God. So Jesus was saying that whoever loves *his existence on earth* loses it; and he who hates *his existence in kosmos* shall keep it to <u>a life in God</u> forevermore.
>
> That statement tests the purity of one's Christian commitment. Culture has a way of corrupting one's Christianity. His outward activities may be "Christian" while his inward allegiance is still in *kosmos*. In our culture, "the preaching of the cross is foolishness." (I Corinthians 1:18) To the "many" who shun the narrow way (Matthew 7:13), the Cross demands too much. It makes no logical sense to them because they approach Christianity from the mindset of *kosmos*. Beguiled by the low level of consecration they see around them, they protest inwardly, "Aren't the sacrifices I've made enough? I've given up drinking, cussing, and fornicating. I 'deny myself' every Sunday morning by going to church when I feel like sleeping in." *But they have never been to Calvary <u>inwardly</u> where their old life has been crucified and a new life has begun.* Real surrender occurs when we choose the narrow way of the Cross. That's when the deep changes begin.
>
> On the other hand, the few (Matthew 7:14) who have gone to Calvary see life eternal at the end of the narrow road. It changes the way they view this life. The temporal yields to the eternal. The inconsequential is replaced by the supremely important. This inward change has enabled saints down through the centuries to face hardship, opposition, persecution, and death. They lived out their Christian testimony in the environs of *kosmos*, but saw themselves as pilgrims in it, not citizens of it. We too must hate our lives in this world, as Jesus said we must. The book of Revelation reveals the fact that those who "overcome" the spirit of Antichrist "loved not their lives unto the death." (Revelation 12:11 KJV)[3]

Friday

1. Read and meditate on Philippians 1:21-30 (supplemental reading: I Thessalonians 1).

2. Write out Philippians 1:30.

3. Look up the word *conflict* (Gk. *agon*[73]) in a Bible dictionary and list some of the synonyms provided.

   a.   b.

   c.   d.

4. Now look up this word's close cousin, *agonizomai*[75], in a Bible dictionary and list some of its synonyms as well.

   a.   b.

   c.   d.

5. Look up the following verses and describe what you learn from these two words.

   Luke 13:24

   Colossians 1:29

   Colossians 2:1

   I Timothy 4:10

   II Timothy 4:7

   Hebrews 12:1

Saturday

1. Read and meditate on Philippians 1 (supplemental reading: I Thessalonians 2).

2. Review the passage from *Intoxicated with Babylon* in Monday's homework (question 4). Carefully examine your life. How detached from the "world" are you really in your daily life? For instance, what are the main things you do in your free time? Explain what are the true "treasures" (Matthew 6:19) of your life.

3. Review the passage from *Intoxicated with Babylon* in Thursday's homework (question 3). If Jesus were to look at your life in light of what He said in John 12:25, what would He find? Explain your answer.

4. In yesterday's homework, we saw the tremendous battle Paul waged for others. First, he did everything within his power to win lost souls to Christ. Then, once they had surrendered their lives to Christ, he fought for them at the throne of God—interceding for their spiritual growth. His entire life was devoted to the spiritual well-being of other people.

    We are called to be "soldiers of Christ." Do you know what it is like to agonize for others in prayer? Do you regularly get out of your "comfort zone" to reach the lost or to help others? Describe the spiritual conflict going on in your daily life for the sake of souls.

Sunday

LOVE AND EARNEST LABOR
Supplemental Reading: Acts 17
Time Frame: 52 A.D.

After the mixed blessings of Philippi—being beaten with rods but seeing the birth of yet another church—the small band of men started off on the 100-mile walk to Thessalonica. There, as he had so many times before, Paul opened his campaign by preaching to the Jews in the local synagogue. They were in the Macedonian city for three Sabbaths—anywhere from two to four weeks—when revival and persecution both broke out simultaneously. Some of the Jews came to the Lord "along with a large number of the God-fearing Greeks." (Acts 17:4)

Paul's sudden, dramatic success infuriated the Jews, who formed a mob with some local troublemakers and attacked the house in which he had been staying. Once again, he was forced to leave town, setting out for the nearby town of Berea. Here he enjoyed a similar, albeit short-lived, success, as troublesome Jews following him from Thessalonica caused him to quietly slip away alone.

When, some time later, he eventually got settled in Corinth, Paul wrote a letter to the new believers in Thessalonica. This short epistle offers a rare glimpse into the great loving heart of this man. Read some of the things he expressed to this congregation whom he came to love dearly during his short time with them:

- Having so fond an affection for you (2:8)
- We were well-pleased to impart to you our own lives, because you had become very dear to us (2:8)
- We were all the more eager with great desire to see your face (2:17)
- We wanted to come to you yet Satan thwarted us (2:18)
- For who is our hope or joy or crown of exultation? Is it not even you? (2:19)
- For you are our glory and joy (2:20)
- When I could endure it no longer, I also sent to find out about your faith (3:5)
- We also long to see you (3:6)
- Now we really live, if you stand firm in the Lord (3:8)
- All the joy with which we rejoice before our God on your account (3:9)
- We night and day keep praying most earnestly that we may see your face (3:10)

Meanwhile, a resolute Paul journeyed alone to Athens, the philosophical capital of the world. The most prolific thinkers and orators of the day congregated there—spending endless hours in futile debate over every new idea that came along.

Apparently, Paul's message was not well-received in the local synagogue so before long he shifted his attention to the Agora—the marketplace. One day, he was preaching to the passing crowds there when a group of Epicurean and Stoic philosophers began debating with him. "What would this idle babbler wish to say?" some questioned. Others chimed in, "He seems to be a proclaimer of strange deities." (Acts 17:18) They decided to bring him to the Aereopagus, where he could share his beliefs with the city's leading philosophers.

The Aereopagus (aka Mars' Hill) was an off-shoot of the Acropolis, the steep precipice in the central city on which the Parthenon and other important buildings had been constructed. Popular legend said that it was on this hillside that the Greek god Aeres (Roman name Mars) was tried for killing another deity by a council of twelve gods; hence its name. Over the years, the council of sages that met there took on the name until, eventually, the Aereopagus became more known for the assembly than for the location which hosted it.*

Paul began his message to this venerated group of men by ingeniously referring to their altar to *An Unknown God*. "What you worship in ignorance, this I proclaim to you," he offered. "The God who made the world and all things in it, since He is Lord of heaven and earth, does not dwell in temples made with hands; nor is He served by human hands, as though He needed anything, since He Himself gives

---

* A modern parallel to this is Wall Street, a tiny lane in Manhattan whose name has long-since become synonymous with and made famous by the financial institution located there.

to all *people* life and breath and all things; and He made from one *man* every nation of mankind to live on all the face of the earth, having determined *their* appointed times and the boundaries of their habitation, that they would seek God, if perhaps they might grope for Him and find Him, though He is not far from each one of us; for in Him we live and move and exist, as even some of your own poets have said, 'For we also are His children.'" (Acts 17:23-28)

Paul, in a passion for these intellectuals' souls, had their undivided attention. They had probably never heard anyone expound on this particular deity with such unshakeable confidence. The earnest preacher poured his heart out to these cynical men. But, when he mentioned the resurrection of Jesus, they erupted into open derision and laughter. "We shall hear you again concerning this," they said, dismissing him as an incompetent amateur.

With that, the discouraged minister left the great city which, like Antioch and so many others he had visited, considered itself "unworthy of eternal life" (Acts 13:42), and headed for the wicked city of Corinth.

WEEK 7: SERVANT OF GOD

Monday

1. Read and meditate on Philippians 2 (supplemental reading: I Thessalonians 3).

2. Write out Philippians 2:3-4.

3. Read the following passage from my book *Irresistible to God* and explain what you learn.

> One essential aspect of humility is living in the constant awareness of the importance of other people. As a believer becomes involved in the lives of others, he becomes less consumed with himself. Conversely, the prideful person is preoccupied with self. His thinking almost always revolves around his own opinions, desires, and needs. Socially, he really is only concerned with himself and his own family. There is very little room left for anybody else because he is so huge in his own mind. Rather than serve others, he seeks to be served.
>
> On the other hand, the humble believer matures out of that selfish thinking and becomes interested in other people. As self-consciousness decreases, he becomes increasingly aware of "the interests of others." Their lives take up a greater part of his consciousness, and he becomes smaller in his own mind. Humility is living with a great concern about the well-being of others and allowing their interests, needs, struggles, dreams, and fears to play a big part in one's own life.[1]

4. Look up the word translated as *more important* (Gk. *huperecho*[5242]) in a Bible dictionary and describe what you learn.

Monday - *continued*

5. Review yesterday's narrative on the life of Paul. Explain what you learn regarding the importance he placed on the lives of others.

6. Read I John 3:17 and explain what you learn about serving the needs of others.

Tuesday

1. Read and meditate on Philippians 2 (supplemental reading: I Thessalonians 4).

2. Rewrite Philippians 2:6-7 in your own words.

3. Jesus left His position at the right hand of God in glory to live on earth serving the needs of others. In the world, a bond-servant is the lowest position, but in the kingdom of God, it is the highest. Look up the following verses and explain what you learn about serving and being a servant.

   Matthew 6:24

   Matthew 10:24-25

   Matthew 20:28

   Matthew 24:45-51

Tuesday - continued

Matthew 25:14-30

Mark 10:42-45

John 13:13-17

Galatians 5:13-14

II Timothy 2:24

Revelation 7:3

Revelation 11:18

Wednesday

1. Read and meditate on Philippians 2 (supplemental reading: I Thessalonians 5).

2. Review Philippians 2:8. Jesus lived His life on earth in utter submission to His heavenly Father. However, all humans have a fallen will which must be broken and conquered to be brought under the yoke of Christ. Christianity means much more than a mere outward obedience to rules. True submission occurs when a person obeys his master from his heart. Read the story in Matthew 21:28-31 and explain what you learn.

3. Read the following passage from my book *Irresistible to God* and explain in detail what you learn.

    The word submit (Gk. *hupotasso*) is a conjunction of two other words: *hupo*, which means "under" and *tasso*, which means "to arrange," thus, "to be arranged under or in subjection to the leadership of another." The best illustration of it is an army assembled in marching formation. Every man is submitted to his superiors.

    However, imagine there was one private straggling outside the ranks, walking along at his own pace, sometimes in formation but most of the time just doing his own thing. The general, seeing the self-will and unsubmissiveness in this private's life, could never trust him to follow orders. How would he respond to that soldier if he approached him requesting something? He would probably be so disgusted with his willfulness and audacity that he would simply walk away from him. Wouldn't it be appropriate for the general to *resist* the insubordinate private?

    A good soldier, on the other hand, obeys out of respect and devotion to his leader. He places himself under the leadership of his commander—not only outwardly but also *in his heart*. It is more than simply obeying out of fear of the consequences for disobedience. He is committed to his leader's cause. In reality, he has renounced his own will in favor of that of the general. His attitude has earned him the trust of his superiors, and he is thereby granted a position of responsibility....

    How does the Lord bring an independent person into real submission? The same way the Army transforms a raw recruit into a disciplined fighter: the beginner's self-will must be crushed, and he must learn to align himself with the will of his superior.[2]

Wednesday - *continued*

4. Truthfully, until a person has been broken of his own will, he will never know the joy of Christianity. Look up the following verses and explain what you learn about submission.

Hebrews 12:9

Hebrews 13:17

James 4:7

I Peter 5:5

Thursday

1. Read and meditate on Philippians 2 (supplemental reading: II Thessalonians 1).

2. Review Philippians 2:12-13. Can you see how the Christian life is a cooperative effort between the believer and God? For hundreds of years, Calvinists have argued that God does everything in this relationship; conversely, Arminians have consistently emphasized man's role. Read the following commentary on these verses by A.T. Robertson, a Baptist scholar of the last century. Explain what you learn from this.

> "Not slavish terror, but wholesome, serious caution" (Vincent). "A nervous and trembling anxiety to do right" (Lightfoot). Paul has no sympathy with a cold and dead orthodoxy or formalism that knows nothing of struggle and growth. He exhorts as if he were an Arminian in addressing men. He prays as if he were a Calvinist in addressing God and feels no inconsistency in the two attitudes. Paul makes no attempt to reconcile divine sovereignty and human free agency, but boldly proclaims both.[3]

3. Read II Peter 1:10. Do you see this cooperative effort expressed in this verse? Explain your answer.

 - *continued*

4. A humble approach to Scripture ("My opinions are not the final say on doctrine.") requires a balanced perspective. For instance, Psalm 119 has many expressions of what both God *and* believers do in this relationship. Look up the following verses and write either "God" or "me" next to it when you determine whose effort is being referenced.

Psalm 119:2   Psalm 119:10a

Psalm 119:10b   Psalm 119:11

Psalm 119:29   Psalm 119:32a

Psalm 119:32b   Psalm 119:35a

Psalm 119:36   Psalm 119:37

Psalm 119:38   Psalm 119:45

Psalm 119:59   Psalm 119:60

Psalm 119:101   Psalm 119:112

Psalm 119:116   Psalm 119:124

Psalm 119:133   Psalm 119:154

Friday

1. Read and meditate on Philippians 2 (supplemental reading: II Thessalonians 2).

2. Write out Philippians 2:14-15.

3. Look up the words translated in the NASB as *grumbling* and *disputing* in a Bible dictionary and describe what you learn.

    a. *grumbling* (Gk. *goggusmos*$_{1112}$)

    b. *disputing* (Gk. *dialogismos*$_{1261}$)

4. The NASB translates Philippians 2:15a: "so that you will prove yourselves to be blameless and innocent...." Look up the following OT verses and describe the blessings of being blameless.

    Psalm 37:18-19

    Psalm 84:11

    Proverbs 11:5a

    Proverbs 11:20b

5. Read Philippians 2:3-8 in *The New Living Translation* (provided below) and describe any fresh perspectives you have gained.

    Don't be selfish; don't try to impress others. Be humble, thinking of others as better than yourselves. Don't look out only for your own interests, but take an interest in others, too. You must have the same attitude that Christ Jesus had. Though he was God, he did not think of equality with God as something to cling to. Instead, he gave up his divine privileges; he took the humble position of a slave and was born as a human being. When he appeared in human form, he humbled himself in obedience to God and died a criminal's death on a cross.

Saturday

1. Read and meditate on Philippians 2 (supplemental reading: II Thessalonians 3).

2. It has been said that the amount a person selflessly serves the needs of others reveals the depth of his or her Christianity. In your daily life, how do you demonstrate that others' needs are more important than your own? In what ways are you involved in helping other people?

3. Conduct a thorough and honest evaluation of your own life in light of Matthew 6:24. Would you say that your life revolves more around serving God or serving your own worldly interests? Explain your answer.

4. Read Luke 22:42 and then Matthew 7:21. Would you say that your life is truly submitted to God's will? Or, would you say that you are living out your own will and fitting Him into your life on your own terms? Explain your answer.

EUROPEAN REVIVAL
Supplemental Reading: Acts 18:1-18
Time Frame: 52 - 54 A.D.

Corinth—the very name conjured up images worldwide of lewdness and licentiousness. It was a filthy port city—similar to modern-day Manila or Hong Kong. Its Acro-Corinth, the hill which housed the local temple dedicated to Aphrodite, was home to "1,000 sacred prostitutes." Unquestionably, Corinth was the most depraved city in the Roman Empire. The exhausted apostle now zeroed in on this center of desperate human need as his next target.

Only a few weeks earlier, Paul's body had been traumatized by the beating in Philippi. Then, he was run out of Thessalonica and Berea just as the Lord began moving upon hearts. The laughter of the Athenian philosophers probably still rang in his ears and stung his heart. Entering the Grecian port of Achaia, the depleted Paul was lonely, dejected and, apparently, also somewhat fearful. Just at the right time, the Lord appeared to him in a vision. "Do not be afraid *any longer,* but go on speaking and do not be silent," He encouraged him, "for I am with you, and no man will attack you in order to harm you, for I have many people in this city." (Acts 18:9-10)

This reassurance, along with the arrival of Silas and Timothy from Macedonia, seemed to renew the apostle's energy, and he was soon out in the streets preaching again. In a letter written later to the Corinthians, Paul provided an accurate description of his preaching in that city. Notice what he did and what he did not rely upon:

And when I came to you, brethren, I did not come with superiority of speech or of wisdom, proclaiming to you the testimony of God. For I determined to know nothing among you except Jesus Christ, and Him crucified. I was with you in weakness and in fear and in much trembling, and my message and my preaching were not in persuasive words of wisdom, but in demonstration of the Spirit and of power, so that your faith would not rest on the wisdom of men, but on the power of God. (I Corinthians 2:1-5)

Have you ever wondered how Paul, though weak of body and contemptible of speech (II Corinthians 10:10), had such tremendous results in his preaching? True, hard-hearted Jews and the unteachable Athenian philosophers were closed to his message; nevertheless, nearly everywhere he went he seemed to reap a harvest of souls. Two primary reasons can account for this phenomenon: First, Paul was full of the Holy Spirit and fire. When he spoke, the Lord used his words to disturb people's souls and bring great conviction of sin within their hearts. Second, Gentiles had not become hardened to the Word of God as had the Jews of his day (or modern Americans). The gospel was new and fresh—not yet stale from years of becoming calloused to its message. Indeed, he later wrote that the gospel was "the power of God for salvation." (Romans 1:16)

We know from Church history that when certain elements are in place, revival can quickly break out in a city. The first Christian outpouring happened on the Day of Pentecost in 33 A.D. when 3,000 people got saved after one sermon. Revivals such as this have occurred many, many times during the past 2,000 years. The Lord used John Wesley and George Whitefield to bring about the Great Awakening of the 18th Century. It was said that when Jonathan Edwards gave his famous message, *Sinners in the Hands of an Angry God*, people cried out in terror, clutching at the pews in fear that the floor beneath them would open and there would be nothing to stop them from sliding into hell.* Charles Finney exuded so much power that people would often break down weeping when he entered a room.

Jonathan Goforth, a Presbyterian missionary to China, was involved in the great Korean Revival of 1907. One of the missionaries present described what happened one evening:

Then began a meeting the like of which I had never seen before, nor wish to see again

---

* Skeptics and lifeless religious people have attempted to explain away this sermon by saying that Edwards terrified simple-minded people into conversions. It is just as Paul himself said, "A natural man does not accept the things of the Spirit of God, for they are foolishness to him; and he cannot understand them…." (I Corinthians 2:14)

Sunday - continued

unless in God's sight it is absolutely necessary. Every sin a human being can commit was publicly confessed that night. Pale and trembling with emotion, in agony of mind and body, guilty souls, standing in the white light of their judgment, saw themselves as God saw them. Their sins rose up in all their vileness, till shame and grief and self-loathing took complete possession; pride was driven out, the face of man forgotten. Looking up to heaven, to Jesus whom they had betrayed, they smote themselves and cried out with bitter wailing: "Lord, Lord, cast us not away forever!" Everything else was forgotten, nothing else mattered. The scorn of men, the penalty of the law, even death itself seemed of small consequence if only God forgave.[4]

Many such accounts have been recorded of God's power breaking out amongst people. These divine visitations occur when a sovereign God draws near and moves upon men in a supernatural way.

Surely when the apostle Paul preached it must have resembled these reports. This would explain why he wrote to the Thessalonians: "For our gospel did not come to you in word only, but also in power and in the Holy Spirit and with full conviction." (I Thessalonians 1:5) He also said of his time with the Thessalonians that the word of God "spread rapidly and [was] glorified." (II Thessalonians 3:1)

Paul faced many, many difficulties, but when he began to share the good news of the gospel, God's presence filled the atmosphere and people were deeply moved in their spirits. This was the man the Lord eventually used to bring revival to Europe.

WEEK 8: LOSS OF ALL THINGS

Monday

1. Read and meditate on Philippians 3 (supplemental reading: I Corinthians 15).

2. Write out Philippians 3:7.

3. Summarize Matthew 10:34-39 in one concise statement.

4. Explain in your own words how the attitudes expressed in Philippians 2:21 and Philippians 3:7 differ from each other.

5. In Philippians 3:3b-7, Paul makes his case against putting one's confidence in his own abilities, education, experience, knowledge and so on. Unfortunately, this is typically not the case in today's Church. A Christian leader's charismatic personality, leadership abilities and talent in the pulpit are emphasized while too often little concern is paid to his walk with God. In I Timothy 3:2-4 and 7, Paul lists the 14 qualifications of an overseer (pastor). Out of this list, how many pertain to abilities and how many pertain to godly character?

Monday - *continued*

6. Look up Matthew 7:15-20 and answer the following questions.

    a. According to Matthew 7:15, how do false prophets appear?

    b. Explain what you think Jesus meant in His description of their inner life.

    c. According to Matthew 7:20, how will you be able to discern their character?

    d. Explain what you think Jesus meant when He used the term "fruits."

Tuesday

1. Read and meditate on Philippians 3 (supplemental reading: I Corinthians 16).

2. According to Philippians 3:8, what did Paul consider to be the great reward for the loss of everything upon which his former life had been built?

3. The knowledge of God is a vast spiritual ocean that is available to anyone interested enough to pursue it. Look up the following verses about this subject and explain what you learn.

   Proverbs 2:1-5

   Jeremiah 9:23-24

   Hosea 6:3, 6

   John 17:3

Tuesday - *continued*

II Corinthians 10:5

Colossians 2:2-3

Titus 1:15-16

II Peter 1:2-3

I John 2:3-4

I John 4:7-8

Wednesday

1. Read and meditate on Philippians 3 (supplemental reading: II Corinthians 1).

2. Rewrite Philippians 3:10 as a personal prayer to the Lord.

3. Every born-again believer would agree that the greatest loss a person could experience would be the loss of Christ. However, to some, this means nothing more than missing out on heaven. Paul had a deeper perspective, though. To him, knowing the Lord did not equate with simply going to church on Sunday and escaping hell one day. Paul's daily relationship with God meant more than anything else in life—including comfort. Setting aside the eternal aspect of the Christian life, carefully explain how your life would be different if you were not a believer.

4. The four benefits of suffering loss that Paul describes in Phil. 3:10 are listed below. Explain how losing things of earthly value would help you to experience these benefits more fully in your daily life.

   a. To know Christ in a deeper way;

   b. To experience resurrection power;

   c. To enjoy the privilege of sharing in His sufferings;

   d. To partake in the process of death to self.

Thursday

1. Read and meditate on Philippians 3 (supplemental reading: II Corinthians 2).

2. Rewrite Philippians 3:13-14 in your own words.

3. In Philippians 3:3-7, Paul described all the things from his past that he had once put his confidence in as a man and religious leader. I think it is fair to say that when he writes about forgetting the things of the past in verse 13, he is primarily referring to those things in life that bring about a sense of confidence in *self* rather than in Christ. Wouldn't you agree? Describe the things in your life that you tend to look to for a sense of *self*-worth rather than looking to your relationship to Christ.

4. Look up the term *press on* (Gk. *dioko*[1377]) in a Bible dictionary and describe what you learn.

5. When Jesus revealed Himself to Paul on the Damascus Road, He used this same term. Read Acts 9:4-5 and explain any new insight you gain into Philippians 3:12-14.

Friday

1. Read and meditate on Philippians 3 (supplemental reading: II Corinthians 3).

2. Write out Philippians 3:20.

3. Compare Philippians 3:19 with Colossians 3:1-2 and describe the contrast you find between these verses.

4. True born-again Christians have become citizens of the kingdom of heaven. Read the following passage from my book *Intoxicated with Babylon* and describe in your own words what this citizenship means to you.

> When someone wishes to immigrate to the United States and become a citizen, he must file the proper applications, take needed tests, and go for interviews – all of which are a part of the necessary procedure. The applicant is also expected to renounce his loyalties to his former country and pledge allegiance to his new homeland.
>
> Some come to America, of course, to use her for their own selfish ambitions and purposes. An example of this occurred in 1979 when Iranian revolutionaries took a number of our diplomats hostage. During that time, patriotism rose to a fever pitch in America. Most of the Iranians who had immigrated to the United States prior to this incident also felt badly about what happened in their former country. Their loyalties lay properly with their new country.
>
> Some Iranian immigrants, however, openly expressed their sympathy for the hostage-takers. The response of patriotic Americans was predictable and right. If these immigrants were in America by our government's good graces; if America had opened its heart and land to them; if they were attending our finest colleges on scholarships; if they were employed at a level unimaginable in Iran; then how could they show sympathy for America's enemies? Where was the gratitude for the bounty of freedoms and opportunities they had been afforded?
>
> But is this not a fair analogy for those who have been allowed entrance into the Kingdom of God, only to withhold their loyalty to it and blatantly disregard the grace, which let them in?... This world is *not* home for the follower of Christ. Christians must be like the American diplomats in Iran during the hostage crisis, continuing to hold their American perspectives and values though in the apparent power of their captors. They still had a job to do, and their loyalties were to their home country.[1]

Saturday

1. Read and meditate on Philippians 3 (supplemental reading: II Corinthians 4).

2. Reconsider the verses you looked up in question 3 of Tuesday's homework. How much of your attention is really focused upon knowing God in a greater way? Explain your answer.

3. Look again at question 4 of Wednesday's homework. Have you ever had a painful experience that brought about any of these spiritual benefits? Explain your answer.

4. Read the passage from *Intoxicated with Babylon* in yesterday's homework. Take an honest inventory of the free (nonworking) time of your daily life. How much of it is really focused on the things of God and how much of it is consumed with the things of this world? Explain your answer.

IN THE SHADOW OF ARTEMIS
Supplemental Reading: Acts 18:18-19:41
Time Frame: 54 - 57 A.D.

Sunday

After a long, grueling campaign in Corinth, Paul, accompanied by Timothy, Silas, Priscilla and Aquilla, and now a new companion named Titus, set sail for Ephesus on one of the many ships that connected the two regional financial centers. The burgeoning little band stopped long enough in Ephesus for Paul to preach once in the synagogue. Even though the Ephesian Jews entreated him to stay longer, he felt compelled to return to his home church in Syrian Antioch. So, leaving Priscilla and Aquilla there to birth and cultivate a new work, the rest of them sailed to Antioch.

Had Paul then known it would be the last time he would set foot in Antioch, perhaps he would have stayed longer. Eventually, though, concerns for all his spiritual children abroad compelled him to leave the comparative comfort and safety of Antioch and embark upon another mission of mercy.

His ultimate destination was Asia, on the western edge of what is now modern-day Turkey. Even though it would have been much quicker to make the 600-mile trip by boat, Paul was anxious to visit the churches in Galatia. So, before long, the small troop set off on foot through the Cilician Gates and back into the territory of Timothy's childhood. They traveled from city to city, strengthening the brethren, before turning west toward Asia.

At that time, three chief cities lay in the province of Asia: picturesque Smyrna, politically powerful Pergamos, and Ephesus, whose one great function and aim was commercialism.

The outstanding feature of Ephesus was clearly the great Temple of Artemis. Local businessmen eagerly perpetuated the belief that the worship of this famous goddess secured divine favor upon one's finances. The Hellenistic temple was so magnificent that it was considered one of the Seven Wonders of the Ancient World.

It was in the ominous shadow of this shrine—both literally and figuratively—that Paul now devoted his latest evangelical efforts. As always, he began in the local synagogue, where, astoundingly, he was allowed to preach undisturbed for three months before his message was rejected. At that point, he began utilizing a local meeting hall to teach those interested in hearing more about Christianity. "This took place for two years, so that all who lived in Asia heard the word of the Lord, both Jews and Greeks." (Acts 19:10)

It's striking that Luke could make such a wide-sweeping statement. Apparently, Paul's disciples fanned out preaching the gospel in cities across Asia—Pergamos, Smyrna, Sardis, Thyatira, Hieropolis, Colossae, Philadelphia and Laodicea. His adherents copied his method of preaching in the local marketplaces where "all" regularly came to acquire fresh provisions. Thus, small churches began popping up across the entire region during Paul's stay in Ephesus. Little wonder that he told the Corinthians that "a wide door for effective *service* has opened to me, and there are many adversaries." (I Corinthians 16:9)

"God was performing extraordinary miracles by the hands of Paul, so that handkerchiefs or aprons were even carried from his body to the sick, and the diseases left them and the evil spirits went out." (Acts 19:12) The Lord was moving mightily through Paul's life and those around him.

Equally true is the fact that he continually faced many difficulties and hardships. During his stay in Ephesus, he wrote his first epistle to the church at Corinth. In it, he poignantly described himself and his helpers as being:

- hungry and thirsty
- poorly clothed
- roughly treated
- homeless

He also mentioned in this letter that he "fought with wild beasts at Ephesus." Right after leaving Ephesus he wrote: "For we do not want you to be unaware, brethren, of our affliction which came *to us* in Asia, that we were burdened excessively, beyond our strength, so that we despaired even of life." (II Corinthians 1:8)

In the face of all of these hardships, Paul and

Sunday - continued

his followers maintained a very sweet spirit. He went on to say that, "when we are reviled, we bless; when we are persecuted, we endure; when we are slandered, we try to conciliate; we have become as the scum of the world, the dregs of all things, *even* until now." (I Corinthians 4:11-13)

During this same time, he wrote the following immortal words that have comforted weary saints throughout the ages: "*We are* afflicted in every way, but not crushed; perplexed, but not despairing; persecuted, but not forsaken; struck down, but not destroyed; always carrying about in the body the dying of Jesus, so that the life of Jesus also may be manifested in our body. For we who live are constantly being delivered over to death for Jesus' sake, so that the life of Jesus also may be manifested in our mortal flesh." (II Corinthians 4:8-11)

Not only was Paul continually exerting efforts at winning the lost, but he was also doing his utmost to build up the saints. Later, he told the Ephesian elders, "You yourselves know, from the first day that I set foot in Asia, how I was with you the whole time, serving the Lord with all humility and with tears and with trials which came upon me through the plots of the Jews; how I did not shrink from declaring to you anything that was profitable, and teaching you publicly and from house to house… remembering that night and day for a period of three years I did not cease to admonish each one with tears." (Acts 20:18-31)

Unquestionably, this extended stay in Asia was one of Paul's most fruitful periods. However, it was at this time that he first began to set his sights upon Rome, desiring to minister in the great seat of Roman power. First, however, he had to deal with some alarmingly unexpected business elsewhere.

WEEK 9: PEACE AND JOY

Monday

1. Read and meditate on Philippians 4:1-9 (supplemental reading: II Corinthians 5).

2. Write out Philippians 4:4.

3. Explain the spiritual truth Nehemiah touched upon when he said, "The joy of the Lord is your strength." (Nehemiah 8:10) In what way does it strengthen the believer?

4. Read and meditate upon the following passage from the *Pulpit Commentary*, then describe what you learn.

> God has joy. He is not indifferent, nor is he morose; we are to think of him as the "blessed" God, *i.e.* as essentially happy. The brightness and beauty of the world are reflections from the blessedness of God. Because he is glad, nature is glad, flowers bloom, birds sing, young creatures bound with delight. Nothing is more sad in perversions of religion than the representations of God as a gloomy tyrant. Less terrible, but scarcely less false, are those monkish ideas which deny the tyranny but cherish the gloom of a somber divinity more suited to chill, dark cloisters than to that glorious temple of nature in which the eternal presence dwells and manifests himself symbolically. These fragrant meadows, broad rolling seas of moorland heather, rich green forest cities of busy insect life, flashing ocean waves, and the pure blue sky above, and all that is sweet and lovely in creation, swell one symphony of gladness, because the mighty Spirit that haunts them is himself overflowing with joy. Our God is a *Sun*. And if divinity is sunny, so should religion be. The happy God will rejoice in the happiness of his children. Innocent mirth, though forbidden by Puritan sourness, can be no offence to such a God. The typical citizens of his kingdom are little children; and what is so joyous as childhood?[1]

Tuesday

1. Read and meditate on Philippians 4:1-9 (supplemental reading: II Corinthians 6).

2. Write out Philippians 4:5.

3. Look up the word *gentle* (Gk. *epieikes*[1933]) in a Bible dictionary and describe what you learn.

4. Compare the different Bible translations provided below with your own translation of Philippians 4:5a. What fresh concepts are revealed to you through these translations?

   a. (AMP) Let all men know and perceive and recognize your unselfishness (your considerateness, your forbearing spirit).

   b. (GNB) Show a gentle attitude toward everyone.

   c. (KJV) Let your moderation be known unto all men.

   d. (NLT) Let everyone see that you are considerate in all you do.

Tuesday - continued

5. Rewrite Philippians 4:6-7 in your words.

6. The two statements found in Philippians 4:6-7 form a conditional promise. In this case there are two conditions. Briefly describe in your own words the promise and the accompanying conditions.

   Promise:

   Condition # 1:

   Condition # 2:

Wednesday

1. Read and meditate on Philippians 4:1-9 (supplemental reading: II Corinthians 7).

2. Write out Philippians 4:9.

3. Compare Philippians 4:9 with II Timothy 2:2 and describe what you learn.

4. Think about Paul's different visits to Philippi (Acts 16:11-40; 20:1-6; II Corinthians 2:13; 7:5; I Thessalonians 2:2) What "things" do you think they "learned and received and heard and (saw) in" him that he implored them to emulate?

5. Look up the word *practice* (Gk. *prasso*$_{4238}$) in a Bible dictionary and describe what you learn.

Wednesday - continued

6. Look up the following verses and describe what you learn about this word.

John 5:29

Romans 1:32

II Corinthians 5:10

II Corinthians 12:21

Galatians 5:19-21

Thursday

1. Read and meditate on Philippians 4:10-23 (supplemental reading: II Corinthians 8).

2. Read Philippians 4:11-12 and I Timothy 6:6-10. Using your own words, summarize both passages in one statement.

3. Write out Philippians 4:13.

4. Considering the context, explain what you think Paul meant in Philippians 4:13.

5. One must always consider context when evaluating the true meaning of a biblical statement. However, such expressions may also stand alone. Philippians 4:13 is a good example of a statement that means one thing in its context but also contains a more general truth as well. The following verses offer similar declarations of faith. For each verse listed below, briefly describe the context and meaning of what is written.

    Numbers 11:23

    Jeremiah 32:27

    Matthew 19:26

    Mark 9:23

    Luke 1:37

Friday

1. Read and meditate on Philippians 4:10-23 (supplemental reading: II Corinthians 9).

2. Write out Philippians 4:19.

3. If there's one thing that is abundantly clear in Scripture, it is God's inclination toward and affinity for the afflicted, poor, and downtrodden of this world. God is irresistibly drawn to the needy. Look up the following verses and describe what you learn.

   I Samuel 2:8

   Psalm 12:5

   Psalm 69:33

   Psalm 72:12-14

   Psalm 107:41

   Isaiah 25:4

4. Read Philippians 4:5-8 in *The New Testament in Modern English* (provided below) and write out what fresh insights or perspectives you gain.

   Have a reputation for gentleness, and never forget the nearness of your Lord. Don't worry over anything whatever; tell God every detail of your needs in earnest and thankful prayer, and the peace of God which transcends human understanding, will keep constant guard over your hearts and minds as they rest in Christ Jesus. Here is a last piece of advice. If you believe in goodness and if you value the approval of God, fix your minds on the things which are holy and right and pure and beautiful and good.

Saturday

1. Read and meditate on Philippians 4 (supplemental reading: II Corinthians 10).

2. Reread the commentary found in Monday's homework. Do you feel that you have the joy of the Lord in your life? Or, do you feel that your joy is determined by favorable circumstances? Explain your answer.

3. Look back at the phrases in question 4 of Tuesday's homework. Do you think that those around you would describe you in such terms? Do you think others perceive you as being joyful in life? Explain your answer.

4. Review Philippians 4:8. Look up each of the following terms in a Bible dictionary and write a couple of synonyms for each. Once you have completed that task, describe how your daily thought life compares to the overall mindset expressed by Paul in Philippians 4:8.

   a. *true* (Gk. *alethes*$_{227}$)

   b. *honorable* (Gk. *semnos*$_{4586}$)

   c. *right* (Gk. *dikaios*$_{1342}$)

   d. *pure* (Gk. *hagnos*$_{53}$)

   e. *lovely* (Gk. *prosphiles*$_{4375}$)

   f. *good repute* (Gk. *euphemos*$_{2163}$)

TROUBLES, PROBLEMS, AND QUESTIONS
Supplemental Reading: II Corinthians 11
Time Frame: 55 - 57 A.D.

Sunday

Paul's ministerial efforts during his three years in Ephesus were not confined to the province of Asia. He was equally concerned about other congregations—not the least of which was the fellowship in Corinth. During the early part of his stay in Ephesus, Apollos returned from Corinth bringing news of the church's condition. Sometime later, a letter from the Corinthian church arrived with questions about different issues that had arisen:

- Should a husband and wife stop having sex to be more spiritual?
- Should a believer divorce his or her unbelieving mate?
- Is it acceptable for a man to give his daughter in marriage?
- Is it permissible to buy meat from the market that had been offered to idols?
- What about the gifts of the Spirit? Are some greater than others?
- Should they speak in tongues before the whole church?

Interestingly, there didn't seem to be any inquiries of the type one would expect from sincere believers. "Paul, tell us how we can draw nearer to God!" "Can you teach us how to walk in the Spirit?" "How can we be more loving to each other?" While the questions they posed were not necessarily out of line, they were certainly of secondary importance.

As Paul mulled over their letter, a delegation arrived from the church that met in Chloe's house in Cenchrea, the port town a few miles from Corinth. They had become disturbed over what they had witnessed in their sister church: divisions, factions, strife and a general lack of love amongst the members. But not only this, there were professing Christians living in open immorality!

Paul, obviously distressed by what he heard and read, sat down and penned the open letter to this church that has become known as First Corinthians. In it, he wanted to provide clear direction to some of the doctrinal issues that had arisen, but more

importantly, he knew he had to confront the sin and strife running rampant in their midst.

Not long after sending this letter, Paul decided it would probably be wise to make a personal appearance there. He anxiously jumped on one of the trans-Aegean ships. During his brief stay, the apostle of love appealed to them in a spirit of humility and meekness, hoping and praying that they would respond. Unfortunately, when a spiritual leader deals humbly with problems, people often rise up in exactly the opposite spirit—pride. Some of the fallacious statements made about him were:

- He was not an apostle (I Corinthians 9:2);
- Therefore, he should not receive financial support (I Corinthians 9:3-14);
- He was unstable and untrustworthy (II Corinthians 1:17-19);
- He was "out of it" (literally: insane) (II Corinthians 5:13); and,
- He was walking in the flesh (II Corinthians 10:2).

In addition, they clamored, "His letters are weighty and strong, but his personal presence is unimpressive and his speech contemptible." (II Corinthians 10:10) Based on what we have previously seen, their criticisms of Paul were not altogether unfounded. He clearly did not preach the gospel there "with superiority of speech or of wisdom" or with "persuasive words of wisdom." (I Corinthians 2:1, 4)

These carnal believers were making a tragically common mistake—judging a man by his outward appearance and personal abilities rather than the degree to which he was possessed of the Holy Spirit. The following ancient account of his appearance may help explain why immature people had such a difficult time respecting him:

St. Paul is set before us as having the strongly marked and prominent features of a Jew... His stature was diminutive, and his body disfigured by some lameness or

Sunday - *continued*

distortion, which may have provoked the contemptuous expressions of his enemies. His beard was long and thin. His head was bald. The characteristics of his face were, a transparent complexion, which visibly betrayed the quick changes of his feelings, a bright gray eye under thickly overhanging united eyebrows, a cheerful and winning expression of countenance, which invited the approach and inspired the confidence of strangers.[2]

When Paul received word that, after he left, many of the Corinthians had risen up in pride and attacked him, he wrote a second letter, which was extremely confrontive.* Sending it ahead with Titus by ship, he traveled up to Troas to await his return. Shortly thereafter, Paul impatiently traveled on to Philippi and met him there. To his relief, Titus brought good news: the people had repented! Then and there, probably in Lydia's house, he sat down and wrote the book of Second Corinthians. Sometime after this letter's arrival among these penitents, Paul arrived in Corinth and spent three months there ministering to the brethren. In the interim, though, there were still unreached areas where lost souls needed to hear the Good News.

---

* The Lord has seen fit to allow this epistle to be lost to us today, probably for good reason.

WEEK 10: SAVED, SUBMITTED AND UNITED

Monday

1. Read and meditate on Colossians 1:1-12 (supplemental reading: II Corinthians 12).

2. Paul's epistle to the believers at Colossae was written about the same time he wrote the book of Ephesians. This fact is further substantiated by the number of similarities found in these two epistles. Look up the following couplings of Scriptures and briefly explain what they share in common.

   a. Ephesians 2:1-5 and Colossians 1:21-23

   b. Ephesians 2:11-18 and Colossians 2:11-15

   c. Ephesians 3:7 and Colossians 1:25

   d. Ephesians 3:9-10 and Colossians 1:26-27

   e. Ephesians 4:22-24 and Colossians 3:9-10

   f. Ephesians 5:19-20 and Colossians 3:16-17

Monday - *continued*

  g. Ephesians 5:21-25 and Colossians 3:18-19

  h. Ephesians 6:1-9 and Colossians 3:20-4:1

  i. Ephesians 6:19 and Colossians 4:3

  j. Ephesians 6:21-22 and Colossians 4:7-8

3. In what way does seeing these similarities give you a greater comprehension of each epistle?

Tuesday

1. Read and meditate on Colossians 1:1-12 (supplemental reading: II Corinthians 13).

2. According to Colossians 1:6, what is "the word of truth, the gospel" doing in "the world?"

3. Read Matthew 13:33. Explain this short parable in light of Colossians 1:6.

4. Rewrite Colossians 1:9 in your own words.

5. On Monday of Week Two, you looked up the Greek term *thelema*[2307] in a Bible dictionary and considered its usage in Ephesians 1. Nevertheless, go ahead and look it up again; this time, list some of the synonyms provided.

   a.   b.

   c.   d.

6. Now look up the following verses and describe what you learn about this word.

   Matthew 7:21

Tuesday - continued

Matthew 12:46-50

Matthew 26:39

Luke 12:47-48

I Thessalonians 4:3-4

I Thessalonians 5:16-18

Hebrews 10:36

I John 2:17

Wednesday

1. Read and meditate on Colossians 1:1-12 (supplemental reading: Galatians 3).

2. Examine Paul's prayers in Ephesians 1:17-19, Ephesians 3:16-19 and Colossians 1:9-12. Extract and combine phrases from these three prayers to create one complete prayer that you can use as a model to intercede for other people in the future. I will provide the beginning and you complete it:

Lord, I ask you to:

1) give him a spirit of wisdom and of revelation in the knowledge of God.

2) enlighten the eyes of his heart so that he may know
   a. what is the hope of Your calling,
   b. what are the riches of the glory of Your inheritance in the saints,
   c. and what is the surpassing greatness of Your power toward us who believe.

Thursday

1. Read and meditate on Colossians 1:13-29 (supplemental reading: Galatians 4).

2. Write out Colossians 1:13-14.

3. Read the following commentary on these verses by Alexander MacLaren and explain what you learn.

> But we must not overlook the significant words in which the condition of possessing this redemption is stated: "in Whom." There must be a real living union with Christ, by which we are truly "in Him" in order to [affirm] our possession of redemption. "Redemption through His blood" is not the whole message of the Gospel; it has to be completed by "In Whom we have redemption through His blood." That real living union is effected by our faith, and when we are thus "in Him," our wills, hearts, spirits joined to Him, then, and only then, are we borne away from "the kingdom of the darkness" and partake of redemption. We cannot get His gifts without Himself.[1]

4. Examine the following verses and briefly explain in your own words what they say about Christ.

Colossians 1:13

Colossians 1:14

Colossians 1:15

Colossians 1:16

Colossians 1:17

Colossians 1:18

Colossians 1:19

Colossians 1:20

Friday

1. Read and meditate on Colossians 1:13-29 (supplemental reading: Galatians 5).

2. Read Colossians 1:21-23 and answer the following questions.

    a. According to Colossians 1:21, what were you formerly?

    b. According to Colossians 1:22, why did Christ reconcile you?

    c. According to Colossians 1:23, what is the *condition* of this reconciliation?

3. The word *if* in the New Testament often expresses *conditions* of salvation. Look up the following verses and explain what you learn.

    John 8:51

    John 15:6-7

    Romans 11:20-22

    II Timothy 2:12

    Hebrews 3:6

    Hebrews 3:14

    Hebrews 10:26

    Hebrews 10:38

    II Peter 2:20

    I John 2:3

Saturday

1. Read and meditate on Colossians 1:1-29 (supplemental reading: Galatians 6).

2. Briefly review the verses you looked up in question 6 of Tuesday's homework, and write out a statement in your own words regarding God's will for your life. Be as detailed as you can and don't be too concerned about grammar here!

3. In your own words, rewrite Paul's prayer in Colossians 1:9-12 as a personal prayer for yourself.

4. Make a list of a) three people who are close to you, and b) three people you don't know very well. Utilize the prayer you created in Wednesday's homework to systematically intercede for each person. This is not meant to become a "canned" prayer but to provide you with God's thoughts in your prayers for these people.

a) Three people close to you:

1.

2.

3.

b) Three people you don't know very well:

1.

2.

3.

ENEMIES WITHIN

Sunday

Supplemental Reading: Acts 20
Time Frame: 57 - 58 A.D.

After Titus left for Corinth, carrying the treasured epistle now known to us as Second Corinthians, Paul himself also departed Philippi and traveled northwest into the region known as Illyricum, along the eastern edge of the Adriatic Sea. Quite possibly he planned to continue on to Rome, but for some reason, he turned southward instead, eventually spending the winter of 57-58 in Corinth.

Paul's ultimate goal was to visit every church he had established to take up an offering for the saints in Judea who were suffering in poverty and famine. First, however, he had more pressing matters to confront: the troublemakers in Corinth who had attempted to turn the church against him.

While most of the church had by this time repented of their immorality, strife and rebellion, apparently there were still those who would not submit to the apostolic authority of Paul. These he undoubtedly dealt with severely, in front of all—leading some to repentance and turning others over to Satan for the destruction of the flesh. No sooner had he dealt with the false brethren in this church than he received painful news from the churches in Galatia. The ever-present Judaisers had made inroads there, fairly successfully turning Paul's converts against him, and rather effectively turning them against the message of grace he preached. They had exchanged the true gospel for "another gospel." They had supplanted faith with works and traded freedom for bondage. The life of the Spirit had been rejected in favor of a fleshly existence. In short, they had retreated back to the Old Testament law, forsaking God's immeasurable grace. In his epistle to them, Paul had a number of strong words to say regarding the Judaisers and their plans for the Galatians:

- They preached a different gospel, distorting the true gospel (1:6-7);
- They were false brethren (2:4);
- They wanted to bring them into bondage (2:4);
- They were hypocrites (2:13);
- They eagerly sought them out to be their followers (4:17);

- They hindered them from obeying the truth (5:7);
- They were troubling and disturbing them (5:10, 12);
- They desired to make a good show in the flesh (6:12).

Not long after Paul wrote to the Galatians, he wrote to the church in Rome. The two epistles have many similarities, leading me to believe that they were probably written about the same time. The primary difference between them is that the letter penned to the Galatians was a personal one, addressed to people Paul knew intimately, while the book of Romans was a formal, doctrinal treatise, ten chapters longer, a veritable "syllabus of the entire Christian and evangelical doctrine." [2]

Throughout Paul's travels, Satan used people to oppose, harass and attack him. The devil most certainly knew that Paul had been entrusted with bringing the gospel to the Gentiles and found plenty of willing accomplices to hinder everything the apostle attempted to accomplish. If he preached in a synagogue, the Jews were incited to guard their national and religious heritage. If he preached in the streets, pagans such as Demetrius in Ephesus were used to attack him. When he brought forth the liberating message of grace, the Judaisers followed behind him to discredit his message. If he attempted to stand for purity and love, there were men like those in Corinth who ridiculed him.

Through it all, Paul continued to stand for truth and yet consistently did so without becoming ugly or even unloving. Jesus had taught, "Love your enemies, do good to those who hate you, bless those who curse you, pray for those who mistreat you." (Luke 6:27-28) Paul consistently lived life in this way. In fact, I could best describe the manner he lived by using his own words: Paul was patient with his enemies. He was kind to those who hated him. He never acted arrogantly or in an unbecoming way toward them. He didn't allow personal interests to take precedence over the needs of others. He was not personally provoked by

Sunday - continued

their mean-spiritedness toward him. And, he didn't take into account wrongs he suffered. (I Corinthians 13:4-5) There were times he had to defend himself, but only because he was concerned that people were being led astray. I'm sure Paul truly loved and prayed for his enemies.

Meanwhile, he had determined to take up an offering for the destitute saints in Jerusalem. He traveled the loop around the Aegean Sea, picking up representatives from each city with their respective donation for the home church. There was Aristarchus from Ephesus, Gaius from Corinth, Tychicus and Trophimus from Asia, as well as others.

Soon Paul and his entourage were on their way back to Palestine. The ship they boarded briefly made port in Miletus, about 35 miles south of Ephesus. Thus, Paul used the occasion to call for the elders of the Ephesian church. He spent valuable time with them—exhorting, encouraging and warning. He exhorted them to be faithful shepherds to their flock. He encouraged them to help the weak and to give to the poor. He warned them that savage wolves would arise from their midst seeking to devour the flock. (Acts 20:17-38) Undoubtedly, he spent many hours on his knees praying for that church. Although wolves did in fact rise up within their ranks, Paul's prayers were heard. Some 40 years later, in a message through John, Jesus commended the Ephesians for enduring in the faith and for discerning false apostles.

Soon, the ship was set to sail and Paul had to part ways with the Asian believers for whom he had developed so much love. The small group was once again on their way to Palestine—into the lion's mouth.

WEEK II: DECEPTIVE PHILOSOPHY

Monday

1. Read and meditate on Colossians 2:1-12 (supplemental reading: Acts 21).

2. Rewrite Colossians 2:3 in your own words.

3. Review Colossians 2:6. Look up the word *walk* (Gk. *peripateo*$_{4043}$) in a Bible dictionary and explain what you learn.

4. Look up the following verses and explain what you learn about this word.

    Romans 8:4

    II Corinthians 5:7

    Galatians 5:16

    Ephesians 2:10

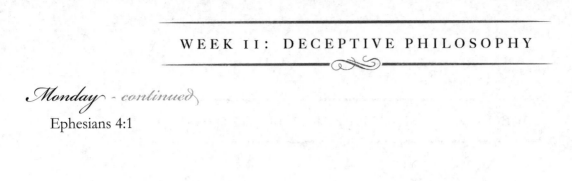

Monday - continued

Ephesians 4:1

Ephesians 5:15

I John 1:6-7

I John 2:6

I John 2:11

II John 1:6

Tuesday

1. Read and meditate on Colossians 2:1-12 (supplemental reading: Acts 22).

2. Write out Colossians 2:6-7.

3. Read the following verses and write out what it means to be *in Christ*.

    Colossians 1:28

    Colossians 2:6

    Colossians 2:7

    Colossians 2:10

    Colossians 2:11

    Colossians 3:3

Tuesday - continued

4. Now read these other verses from the New Testament and write out what it means to be *in Christ*.

John 3:15

John 15:5

Romans 6:11

II Corinthians 5:17

II Thessalonians 1:12

I John 2:5-6

I John 2:28

Wednesday

1. Read and meditate on Colossians 2:1-12 (supplemental reading: Acts 23).

2. Write out Colossians 2:8-10.

3. Read the following passage I wrote and describe your thoughts about the subject being addressed.

Ever since man's earliest days, Satan has used false teachers to introduce deceptive concepts that subtly lead people away from a real relationship to God. In O.T. times, God's rightful position with His people was denigrated by the idea that they could worship Him *and* the popular idols of the day. Jesus had to contend with "the traditions of men" (Mark 7:8) which had gradually supplanted the reality of God with cold formalism. By the end of the First Century, Gnosticism had swept a large percentage of Christians into its heretical fold. During the long history of the Church, each age has faced similar deceptions that gained popularity, albeit short-lived.

The old adage says that hindsight is 20/20. It's easy for us to look back on past deviations from Truth and marvel that the people of that age could be so gullible. But we must understand that, at the time, the enemy had successfully thrown such a false light on the subject that undiscerning people lost their ability to see it for what it really was. Once a particular falsehood gains momentum, it can easily develop into a universal mindset—a belief system that becomes accepted by the majority of that people group. A false belief system can become so enormous, even within the Christian community, that it becomes unassailable.

After twenty years in the counseling field, I am convinced that the greatest falsehood of our age has been introduced into the Church through the multi-faceted system called "Christian" psychology. Using a mixture of commonsense advice, a smattering of Biblical truth and a preponderance of worldly philosophy, "Christian" psychology has subtly and quietly gained more credibility in the minds of unsuspecting believers than even the Word of God. What's worse is that it nearly always leads people away from repentance and the message of the Cross instead of allowing them to experience its transforming power.

Wednesday - continued

4. Read the following passage from Dr. Ed Bulkley's book, *Why Christians Can't Trust Psychology*, and explain what you think the apostle Paul's attitude and thoughts would be toward psychology.

Psychology has offered an alternative to Christianity with a fully developed system of faith…. The Bible claims to reveal the motives of the human heart, while psychology claims to explain the unconscious drives of the human mind. Christianity claims that humans can be transformed by the miraculous and mysterious power of God. Psychology claims that it can transform man by helping him to understand, accept, and love himself.

The Bible says that man is by nature a sinner, separated from the life of God. Psychology says that man is essentially good and needs to recognize his full potential. The Bible says that without Christ, man is hopeless; psychology says that man is limited only by his imagination. The Bible says that man is lost and that Christ is the only way; psychology says it can help man find his own way. The Bible calls sin by name; psychology says that man suffers from disorders….

Down through the centuries, without the aid of psychotherapy or innovative techniques, Christianity has produced millions of permanently transformed lives by the liberating truths found in Jesus Christ. In barely one century, psychology has captured the minds of millions with a message that has enslaved mankind to vacillating theories which promote sinful behavior.

Psychology points man to self. The Bible points man to God.[1]

Thursday

1. Read and meditate on Colossians 2:13-23 (supplemental reading: Acts 24).

2. Read the following commentary about this section of Colossians 2 and explain what you learn.

> We have here the very heart and centre of the practical counsels of the Epistle — the double blasts of the trumpet warning against the two most pressing dangers besetting the Church. They are the same two which we have often met already — on the one hand, a narrow Judaising enforcement of ceremonial and punctilios of outward observance; on the other hand, a dreamy Oriental absorption in imaginations of a crowd of angelic mediators obscuring the one gracious presence of Christ our Intercessor....
>
> The relation of the Gentile converts to these Jewish practices was an all-important question for the early Church. It was really the question whether Christianity was to be more than a Jewish sect — and the main force which, under God, settled the contest, was the vehemence and logic of the Apostle Paul.[2]

3. As we have previously seen, one of the groups of false teachers Paul was concerned about was the Judaisers. In last Sunday's narrative, there is a list of bulleted statements he made to the Galatians about these false teachers. Review those statements and explain, in your own words, Paul's concern for the Colossian church.

4. The other group that was just beginning to make inroads into the Church at this time was the Gnostics. Gnosticism was a strange hybrid of eastern mysticism, Greek philosophy and Christian doctrine. Although its teachings varied greatly amongst its proponents, its foundational premise was that all matter is evil. Out of that understanding came two primary schools of thought. The first espoused that since all matter is evil, Christians should live in severe self-abasement and asceticism. This thinking led to extreme spiritual pride. The other school of thought proposed that since all matter is evil, it doesn't matter what a believer does; he might as well completely indulge his fleshly desires. Reread Colossians 2:13-23. Which form of Gnosticism was Paul addressing in this passage? Explain what else you learn about it in these passages.

Friday

1. Read and meditate on Colossians 2:13-23 (supplemental reading: Acts 25-26).

2. Write out Colossians 2:18.

3. Read the following commentary on this verse and explain what you learn.

> The word used here ("self-abasement" - *tapeinophrosune*) means "lowliness of mind, modesty, humbleness of deportment;" and the apostle refers, doubtless, to the spirit assumed by those against whom he would guard the Colossians—the spirit of modesty or of humble inquirers. The meaning is, that they would not announce their opinions with dogmatic certainty, but they would put on the appearance of great modesty. In this way, they would become really more dangerous—for no false teachers are so dangerous as those who assume the aspect of great humility, and who manifest great reverence for divine things….
>
> *Vainly puffed up by his fleshly mind*—Notwithstanding the avowed "humility," the modesty, the angelic reverence, yet the mind was full of vain conceit, and self-confident, carnal wisdom. The two things are by no means incompatible - the men apparently most meek and modest being sometimes the most bold in their speculations, and the most reckless in regard to the great landmarks of truth.[3]

4. Read Colossians 2:1-4 in *The Amplified Bible* (provided below) and describe any fresh concepts that are revealed to you through each of these verses.

> FOR I want you to know how great is my solicitude for you [*how severe an inward struggle I am engaged in for you*] and for those [*believers*] at Laodicea, and for all who [*like yourselves*] have never seen my face and known me personally.
>
> [*For my concern is*] that their hearts may be braced (comforted, cheered, and encouraged) as they are knit together in love, that they may come to have all the abounding wealth and blessings of assured conviction of understanding, and that they may become progressively more intimately acquainted with and may know more definitely and accurately and thoroughly that mystic secret of God, [*which is*] Christ (the Anointed One).
>
> In Him all the treasures of [*divine*] wisdom (comprehensive insight into the ways and purposes of God) and [*all the riches of spiritual*] knowledge and enlightenment are stored up and lie hidden.
>
> I say this in order that no one may mislead and delude you by plausible and persuasive and attractive arguments and beguiling speech.

Saturday

1. Read and meditate on Colossians 2:1-23 (supplemental reading: Philemon).

2. In questions 3 and 4 of Tuesday's homework, you looked at a number of verses that referred to being *in Christ*. Pick out five of them and apply them to your personal life. Explain what they mean to you and/or how they affect you.

   a.

   b.

   c.

   d.

   e.

3. Look through the Christian books you own and ponder the message of each one, determining whether it is based in the wisdom of God or the wisdom of men. Do you think you should rethink some of the teachings you have accepted down through the years? If so, which ones? Make a list of any Christian books that you have come to see were unbiblical in their teachings. Explain why you feel that way.

INTO THE LION'S MOUTH

Sunday

Supplemental Reading: Acts 27
Time Frame: 58 - 61 A.D.

Trouble was brewing in Palestine. Years of oppression had created a deep-seated hatred amongst the Jewish population for anything "Roman." This was further exacerbated by the brutal reign of Antoninus Felix, the inept procurator of Judea. His philosophy, much like his predecessor Pilate some years before him, was to use force as the first recourse in resolving problems. Within the Jewish community, anti-Gentile feeling was reaching a fever pitch. It was about this time that animosity between the Jewish and Syrian inhabitants of Caesarea broke out into an open battle, which had to be subdued by ruthless Roman might. This underlying social foment culminated in the great revolt that brought about the eventual destruction of Jerusalem in 70 A.D. and the subsequent mass suicide on Masada.

Into this boiling cauldron of hatred for all non-Jews entered the venerable apostle to the Gentiles. Having already known for some time that "bonds and afflictions await[ed]" him, (Acts 20:23) Paul was not surprised when Agabus the prophet warned him that the Jews would "deliver him into the hands of the Gentiles." (Acts 21:11)

Paul and his group made the trip inland from Caesarea up to Jerusalem. While there, some Jews who had debated with him in Ephesus claimed that he had taken Trophimus, an Ephesian Gentile, into the inner court of the temple. A wild mob attacked Paul and would have beaten him to death had not the Roman commander (ironically) detached a garrison to rescue him. It is an amazing testimony to his great heart of love for the unsaved Jews that, after such a traumatic experience, his first thought was still to reach them with the gospel. Receiving permission to speak to them, he began sharing the story about how Jesus had appeared to him on the Damascus road. The incensed Jews reluctantly listened to him—until he said that Jesus had commissioned him to take the gospel to the Gentiles. This was too much for the patriotic Jews. Once again, the crowd erupted into a frenzy, forcing the Romans to rush Paul off to safety.

Upon hearing of a threat on Paul's life by Jewish zealots, Felix had Paul clandestinely transferred to the Roman stronghold in Caesarea. After conducting a puppet trial, Felix had so botched his relations with the Jews that they sent a delegation to Rome to demand his dismissal. By all rights, Felix should have immediately released Paul, but he knew he could not afford to further antagonize the Jews. His solution was to do nothing. Paul was kept detained in comfortable quarters, even being allowed regular visits from his friends. He could easily have been tempted to grow frustrated during this confinement, but he had long since come to realize that a sovereign God was watching over every aspect of his life.

Such a pause in a career of such activity—such an arrest of the Apostle's labours at so critical a time—two years taken from the best part of a life of such importance to the world—would seem to us a mysterious dispensation of Providence, if we did not know that God has an inner work to accomplish in those who are the chosen instruments for effecting His greatest purposes. As Paul might need the repose of preparation in Arabia, before he entered on this career, so his prison at Caesarea might be consecrated to the calm meditation, the less interrupted prayer—which resulted in a deeper experience and knowledge of the power of the Gospel. Nor need we assume that his active exertions for others were entirely suspended. "The care of the churches" might still be resting on him: many messages, and even letters, of which we know nothing, may have been sent from Caesarea to brethren at a distance. And a plausible conjecture fixes this period and place for the writing of St. Luke's Gospel under the superintendence of the Apostle of the Gentiles.[4]

Eventually, Felix's troubles caught up with him and he was replaced by the more evenhanded Porcius Festus. Once situated in his new office, the new

Sunday - continued

procurator summoned Paul to a hearing. The Jews once again spewed forth their accusations against him. Festus, wanting to begin his reign on good footing with the Jews, asked Paul if he were willing to go to Jerusalem to stand trial. The apostle knew only too well how that would end.

In 60 A.D., Claudius Caesar Nero was still widely considered to be a good emperor. So it was not a foolish move on Paul's part to appeal to the emperor. As a Roman citizen, he would be granted his request. He would set sail on the first ship available to the capital of the known world.

However, late fall was not a good time to travel on the Mediterranean Sea as violent storms from the northeast were known to rush in upon hapless ships. After many relatively calm days at sea, this is exactly what happened to the vessel carrying Paul and his companions.

It's not easy for us to imagine how much would be suffered by those involved in a storm like this in ancient times. The strain of both mind and body, the incessant demand for labor battling the storm, the frantic bailing out of water that would rush right back in, retching through it all with violent seasickness, the benumbing effect of the cold and wet, the days of going without food or sleep, and finally, being gripped by terror and hopelessness through it all, was enough to wear out the sturdiest sailor. Paul recounted this and other journeys like it in a later letter to the Corinthians: "dangers on the sea….. in labor and hardship, through many sleepless nights, in hunger and thirst, often without food, in cold and exposure." (II Corinthians 11:26, 27)

And yet it was during this time, when all hope was lost, that the Savior appeared to Paul and assured him that his prayers would be answered: all those aboard would be spared. Finally, having been carried along in the great 'Nor'easter' for two weeks, the ship did not land along some rocky shoreline of Africa where one would expect, but miraculously 480 miles due west on the island of Malta—just south of Rome! And so, after wintering in Malta, Paul finally arrived in the great capital of the Roman Empire in the spring of 61 A.D.

WEEK 12: SEEKING THE THINGS ABOVE

Monday

1. Read and meditate on Colossians 3:1-15 (supplemental reading: I Timothy 1-3).

2. Write out Colossians 3:1.

3. Paul opens the third chapter of Colossians with a dual statement about our new life in Christ. The first relates to Christ's present position in heaven. Look up the following verses and explain what additional information you glean about this glorious truth.

   Psalm 110:1-2

   Mark 16:19

   Acts 7:55-56

   Ephesians 1:20-22

   Hebrews 1:3

   Hebrews 8:1

Monday - *continued*

Hebrews 12:2

Revelations 5:11-14

4. Paul also states in Colossians 3:1 that the believer has been raised up with Christ. Look up the following verses and explain what you learn about our present and eternal relationship to Christ.

John 12:26

John 14:2-3

Romans 6:4-11

Ephesians 2:5-7

Revelation 3:21

Tuesday

1. Read and meditate on Colossians 3:1-15 (supplemental reading: I Timothy 4-6).

2. Rewrite Colossians 3:1-3 in your own words.

3. Read the following commentary from Matthew Henry and follow the directions supplied in the next question.

    He begins with exhorting them to set their hearts on heaven, and take them off from this world: *If you then have risen with Christ.* It is our privilege that we have risen with Christ; that is, have benefit by the resurrection of Christ, and by virtue of our union and communion with him are justified and sanctified, and shall be glorified. Hence he infers that we must *seek those things which are above.* 1) We must mind the concerns of another world more than the concerns of this. 2) We must make heaven our scope and aim, 3) seek the favour of God above, 4) keep up our communion with the upper world by faith, and hope, and holy love, and 5) make it our constant care and business to secure our title to and qualifications for the heavenly bliss....

    To seek heavenly things is to set our affections upon them, to love them and let our desires be towards them. Upon the wings of affection the heart soars upwards, and is carried forth towards spiritual and divine objects. 6) We must acquaint ourselves with them, 7) esteem them above all other things, and 8) lay out ourselves in preparation for the enjoyment of them.[1]

4. Describe, in your own words, each of the 8 things believers must do according to Matthew Henry (numbers supplied).

    1.

    2.

Tuesday - continued

3.

4.

5.

6.

7.

8.

Wednesday

1. Read and meditate on Colossians 3:1-15 (supplemental reading: Titus 1-2).

2. In Colossians 3:5, Paul lists five things believers should be dead to. Look up each of these Greek terms in a Bible dictionary and list some of the synonyms provided.

    a. *immorality* (Gk. *porneia*$_{4202}$):

    b. *impurity* (Gk. *akatharsia*$_{167}$):

    c. *passion* (Gk. *pathos*$_{3806}$):

    d. *evil desire* (Gk. *epithumia*$_{1939}$):

    e. *greed* (Gk. *pleonexia*$_{4124}$):

3. According to Colossians 3:6, why will God's wrath be unleashed?

4. In Colossians 3:8, Paul lists another five things to which believers should be reckoned as dead. Look up each of these Greek terms in a Bible dictionary and list some of the synonyms provided.

    a. *anger* (Gk. *orge*$_{3709}$):

    b. *wrath* (Gk. *thumos*$_{2372}$):

    c. *malice* (Gk. *kakia*$_{2549}$):

    d. *slander* (Gk. *blasphemia*$_{988}$):

    e. *abusive speech* (Gk. *aischrologia*$_{148}$):

5. According to Colossians 3:9, what else should believers not do?

Thursday

1. Read and meditate on Colossians 3:1-15 (supplemental reading: Titus 3).

2. In Colossians 3:12, Paul lists five things believers should *put on*. Look up each of these Greek terms in a Bible dictionary and list some of the synonyms provided.

   a. *compassion* (Gk. *oiktirmos*[3628]):

   b. *kindness* (Gk. *chrestotes*[5544]):

   c. *humility* (Gk. *tapeinophrosune*[5012]):

   d. *gentleness* (Gk. *praotes*[4236]):

   e. *patience* (Gk. *makrothumia*[3115]):

3. According to Colossians 3:13-14, what else should believers do?

4. Read the following quote from my book *Living In Victory* and explain what you learn about the Lord's patience.

   "Longsuffering is that quality of self-restraint in the face of provocation which does not hastily retaliate or promptly punish; it is the opposite of anger and is associated with mercy, and is used of God..." This is why the Lord calls Himself "slow to anger" (Exodus 34:6). When provoked, the Lord does not respond out of the highly charged emotions of the moment, like we humans tend to do. His response is slow, measured, and calculated, and it always goes through the Holy Spirit's filter of love. God is not like the person who says, "I don't get mad, I just get even." He does not get mad or even, at least not in the petulant way humans do.

   Matthew Henry grasped the very motive behind the longsuffering character of God when he said: "It can endure evil and provocation, without being filled with resentment or revenge. It will put up with many slights from the person it loves, and wait long to see the kindly effects of such patience on him."

   For this Being of Love, patiently enduring the abuse of those whom His affections are set upon is simply an unavoidable part of trying to convey that love. In fact, it is not simply something He wishes He could avoid, but is willing to endure; it is something He does joyfully. It is His loving and patient response to our rebellion that makes us love Him all the more. In a sense, He is happy to put up with our slights, knowing one day we will recognize how we have treated Him and it will only serve to increase our love for Him. "But God demonstrates His own love toward us, in that while we were yet sinners, Christ died for us." (Romans 5:8)[2]

Friday

1. Read and meditate on Colossians 3:16-4:18 (supplemental reading: II Timothy 1-2).

2. Rewrite Colossians 3:16 in your own words.

3. Review Colossians 3:17 and 3:23-24 and explain in your own words what Paul is saying here.

4. Write out Colossians 4:2.

5. Read Christ's parable in Luke 18:1-8 and explain what you think it means to be devoted to prayer.

6. Read the following commentary on Luke 18:1 and explain what you learn.

    Always - At all times. That is, we must not neglect regular stated seasons of prayer; we must seize on occasions of remarkable providences as afflictions or signal blessings to seek God in prayer; we must "always" maintain a spirit of prayer, or be in a proper frame to lift up our hearts to God for his blessing, and we must not grow weary though our prayer seems not to be answered.

    Not to faint - Not to grow weary or give over. The parable is designed to teach us that, though our prayers should long appear to be unanswered, we should persevere, and not grow weary in supplication to God.[3]

Saturday

1. Read and meditate on Colossians 3-4 (supplemental reading: II Timothy 3-4).

2. Briefly revisit Ephesians 1-3 and/or its homework (Weeks 1-3). List three things that stand out to you from what God revealed to you, either about His Word or about yourself. Describe how this revelation will help you in your Christian walk in the future.

    a.

    b.

    c.

3. Briefly revisit Ephesians 4-6 and/or its homework (Weeks 4 & 5). List three things that stand out to you from what God revealed to you, either about His Word or about yourself. Describe how this revelation will help you in your Christian walk in the future.

    a.

    b.

    c.

4. Briefly revisit Philippians 1-4 and/or its homework (Weeks 6-9). List three things that stand out to you from what God revealed to you, either about His Word or about yourself. Describe how this revelation will help you in your Christian walk in the future.

    a.

Saturday - continued

    b.

    c.

5. Briefly revisit Colossians 1-4 and/or its homework (Weeks 10-12). List three things that stand out to you from what God revealed to you, either about His Word or about yourself. Describe how this revelation will help you in your Christian walk in the future.

    a.

    b.

    c.

6. Explain how the writings and life of the apostle Paul serves as an exhortation to continue *Pressing On Toward the Heavenly Calling.*

THE FINAL YEARS
Supplemental Reading: Acts 28
Time Frame: 61 - 68 A.D.

Sunday

The praetorian (or imperial) guard was comprised of nine highly-skilled regiments of soldiers, each one thousand strong, whose primary function was to protect the emperor and his interests throughout the empire. Upon his arrival in Rome, "Paul was allowed to stay by himself, with the soldier who was guarding him" in "his own rented quarters." (Acts 28:16, 30) A squadron of soldiers, no doubt hand-picked from a select praetorian phalanx, most likely took turns—in four-hour shifts—chained to the apostle.

One might wonder what it was like for the guard thus assigned to watch this Spirit-filled man. Surely he would have seen, day in and day out, Paul's utterly selfless concern for other people. When other believers would visit Paul, he would have witnessed glorious times of praise and worship. He most certainly would have heard the Word of God expounded upon with great conviction. He probably would have seen devils cast out, indisputable healings and mighty miracles. Surely he would be unable to miss the ever-present glow of love on Paul's face.

Little wonder then that during his stay there, Paul would write: "Now I want you to know, brethren, that my circumstances have turned out for the greater progress of the gospel, so that my imprisonment in *the cause of* Christ has become well known throughout the whole praetorian guard and to everyone else." (Philippians 1:12-13) One can only imagine that many of these veteran soldiers were themselves "rescued from the domain of darkness, and transferred to the kingdom of His beloved Son." (Colossians 1:13)

Through Paul's chains, the good news not only infiltrated the soldiers' ranks, but also became known throughout the vast community of slaves attached to Caesar's household: cooks, housekeepers, maintenance men, dishwashers, and so on. There was also in those days a pitiable group of men and women, boys and girls, kept in the imperial palace for no other reason than to be the objects of Nero's vile and sordid fantasies. They mercifully heard the Gospel as well.

Sometime during this period, Paul wrote three letters in quick succession and sent them off to the province of Asia with Tychicus and Onesimus. The first was a personal appeal to Philemon, written on behalf of Onesimus. Next, he wrote the classic epistle to the churches of Asia, known later as the book of Ephesians. Lastly, he penned a letter to the church in the tiny hamlet of Colossae. Some months later, he followed these up with a letter to his beloved friends in Philippi.

In the spring of 63 A.D., Paul was formally acquitted of all charges. His Jewish accusers, wisely, had failed to show up at his trial, perhaps hearing the rumors of Nero's increasingly bizarre behavior. In July of 64, the emperor set fire to Rome, intending to rebuild it into a magnificent city he would call Neropolis. He may have underestimated the degree of damage that would actually occur, as 11 of its 14 precincts were damaged or destroyed.

Nero, needing a scapegoat for his folly, quickly seized upon public suspicion and animosity toward the Christians to claim that they were the ones guilty of arson. A period of unimaginable horror ensued:

There began a carnival of blood such as even heathen Rome never saw before or since. It was the answer of the powers of hell to the mighty preaching of the two chief apostles, which had shaken heathenism to its centre. A "vast multitude" of Christians was put to death in the most shocking manner. Some were crucified, probably in mockery of the punishment of Christ, some sewed up in the skins of wild beasts and exposed to the voracity of mad dogs in the arena. The satanic tragedy reached its climax at night in the imperial gardens… Christian men and women, covered with pitch or oil or resin, and nailed to posts of pine, were lighted and burned as torches for the amusement of the mob; while Nero, in fantastical dress, figured in a horse race, and displayed his art as charioteer. Burning alive was the ordinary punishment of incendiaries; but only the cruel ingenuity of this imperial monster, under the inspiration of the devil, could invent such a horrible system of illumination.[4]

Some speculate that, just prior to this great tragedy, Paul had accomplished his long-held dream to visit Spain. Sometime later he returned to his old haunts around the Aegean Sea.* He mentions leaving Timothy in Ephesus and traveling on to Macedonia, probably once again staying in the comfortable home of Lydia. (I Timothy 1:3) While there, he wrote his first letter to Timothy.

After that, he and Titus traveled to Crete. He spent some time there, leaving Titus behind. (Titus 1:5) He next traveled back up to Miletus, where he left a sickly Trophimus, heading from there on to Corinth. (II Timothy 4:20) Paul eventually arrived in Nicopolis, where he spent the winter and wrote his epistle to Titus. (Titus 3:12) At some point, he went on to Troas, where he left his cloak and parchments. (II Timothy 4:13) It is very possible that he was suddenly arrested there and had to leave his important items behind.

Before long, Paul was hauled back to Rome, a prized prisoner of Nero. This time, he wouldn't be lodged in rented quarters but in a foul Roman dungeon. While there, he corresponded through one final letter with his beloved Timothy.

It is highly likely that during the spring of 68 A.D., just before the death of Nero, Paul was sentenced to death. Being a Roman citizen, he was spared the torturous and ignominious death of his brethren. In all probability, the end came as a centurion and squadron of soldiers marched him out of the city, and decapitated him with a sword. His last written words serve as a wonderful epitaph to his life:

> "I am already being poured out as a drink offering, and the time of my departure has come. I have fought the good fight, I have finished the course, I have kept the faith; in the future there is laid up for me the crown of righteousness, which the Lord, the righteous Judge, will award to me on that day; and not only to me, but also to all who have loved His appearing." (II Timothy 4:6-8)

---

* There are differences of opinion about how long he lived after this and what he actually did. The provided scenario is speculation based upon meager scraps of information gleaned from Scripture and early Christian writers.

TIMELINE OF THE LIFE OF PAUL

YEAR AD		REFERENCE

SAUL THE PHARISEE

3 ?	• Saul born and spends early years in Tarsus.	Acts 22:3
10 ?	• Saul is sent to Jerusalem at a young age and at some point begins studies under Gamaliel, spending several years at this, becoming a Pharisee.	Acts 22:3
34 ?	• Stephen argues with Hellenistic Jews from Cyrenia, Alexandria, Cilicia and Asia of the Synagogue of the Freedmen; Saul is probably one of these.	Acts 6:9
	• Stephen is stoned; Saul holds the coats of those who stone him.	Acts 8:1; 22:20
	• Saul begins his persecution of the church.	Acts 8:1; 22:4; 26:9-11

SAUL THE NEW CHRISTIAN

36 ?	• Saul has his Damascus Road experience, spending three days blinded until Ananias comes.	Acts 9:1-19; 22:5-16; 26:12-18
	• Saul spends time in Damascus, preaching to the Jews in the synagogue.	Acts 9:19-22
	• Saul is called into Arabia so that God could "reveal His Son in me."	Gal. 1:16-17
36-39	• He returns to Damascus where he continues preaching for the remainder of three years (after his conversion) and the Jews try to kill him. He escapes by night and goes to Jerusalem.	Acts 9:22-29; II Cor. 11:32-33 Gal. 1:18-20
	• In Jerusalem he meets with Peter and the others and begins preaching to the Jews in their synagogues.	Acts 9:29-30
	• The Jews begin trying to put him to death so the apostles send him back to Tarsus. At the same time he has a vision while praying in the temple, the Lord calling him to the Gentiles.	Acts 22:17-21
	• Saul spends some time (prob. preaching) in the regions of Syria and Cilicia.	Gal. 1:21
43	• "Out of body" experience.	II Cor. 12:1-2

THE FIRST MISSIONARY JOURNEY

44-45	• Barnabas comes to Tarsus to take Saul back to Antioch to help with the work there. He spends a year there and then he and Barnabas take an offering to the Jerusalem church.	Acts 11:25-30
44	• Herod Agrippa is struck down by the Lord; Paul and Barnabas return from Jerusalem.	Acts 12:20-25
48	• Paul and Barnabas are sent out from Antioch, traveling to Cyprus where they meet Elymas the magician. Then they sail to Perga, where Mark leaves them. They travel up into the mountains and on to Pisidian Antioch, where they preach to the Jews in the synagogue.	Acts 13:1-3 Acts 13:4-52; II Cor. 11:26 Gal. 4:13-15
	• Next they travel down to Iconium but flee when they learn of a plot to kill them.	Acts 14:1-5
	• Paul and Barnabas travel to Lystra, where Paul heals a man. The people acclaim them as gods but the Jews arrive from Antioch and incite the people to stone Paul.	Acts 14:6-19
	• They leave for Derbe, leading more to Christ there.	Acts 14:20
	• They then return the same way they came, appointing elders in each city.	Acts 14:21-25
50	• Finally, they arrive back in Antioch, where they spend "a long time." Possibly writes Galatians.	Acts 14:26-28
	• Pharisee believers start making trouble so Paul and Barnabas come to Jerusalem to explain what God is doing.	Gal. 2:1-10; Acts 15:1-5
	• Paul and Barnabas appear before the Council and a ruling is made and a letter sent.	Acts 15:6-29
	• Paul and Barnabas return to Antioch.	Acts 15:30-35
51	• Peter visits Antioch and he and Barnabas are rebuked by Paul.	Gal. 2:11-14
	• Paul and Barnabas argue about Mark. Paul separates, taking Silas with him on another trip.	Acts 15: 36-41

THE SECOND MISSIONARY JOURNEY: GALATIA & PHILIPPI

- Paul and Silas travel through Galatia, picking up Timothy along the way. — Acts 16:1-5
- The three travel through Phrygia and Galatia, but are not allowed to preach in Asia. — Acts 16:6
- They enter Mysia but are stopped by the Holy Spirit from going into Bithynia. — Acts 16:7

52
- While in Troas, Paul has a vision of a man from Macedonia asking for help. — Acts 16:8-10
- They travel to Philippi where they lead Lydia and others to the Lord. Paul casts the devil out of the servant girl, whereby a mob grabs Paul and Silas and the magistrates have them beaten with rods and thrown in prison. — Acts 16:11-40

THE SECOND MISSIONARY JOURNEY: THESSALONICA

- The three leave Philippi and travel to Thessalonica where many are saved but a mob rises up and makes Jason give a pledge. — Acts 17:1-10; I The. 1:5-3:13
- They leave Thessalonica and go to Berea. — Acts 17:10-13

THE SECOND MISSIONARY JOURNEY: CORINTH

- Timothy and Silas remain in Berea, Paul leaves for Athens by himself. He preaches at the Areopagos. — Acts 17:14-34

52-54
- Paul journeys to Corinth where he meets and stays with Aquila and Priscilla. Silas and Timothy join him there. Paul preaches at the synagogue, leading Crispus, the leader of the synagogue, to the Lord before the Jews make it impossible for him to preach there any longer. The Lord appears to him in a vision and tells him not to fear, but to stay there. Paul stays there preaching for a year and a half. While there the Jews rise up against Paul and bring him to Gallio who refuses to judge him. The Greeks beat the Jews. — Acts 18:1-18; I Cor. 2:1-5; 16:11
- While in Corinth, Paul pens First and Second Thessalonians.
- Paul, Aquila and Priscilla sail to Ephesus. Paul preaches at the synagogue and the Jews ask him to stay longer. — Acts 18:19-20
- Paul leaves Aquilla and Priscilla in Ephesus and he, Timothy and Silas sail for Palestine. He greets the church in Jerusalem (where he probably leaves Silas) and travels to Antioch. — Acts 18:21-22

THE THIRD MISSIONARY JOURNEY: EPHESUS

- Paul travels through Galatia, "strenghtening the disciples." — Acts 18:23
- Apollos arrives at Ephesus, preaching to the Jews. After some time the brethren send him to Corinth. — Acts 18:24-28

54-57
- Paul and Timothy arrive in Ephesus, where they meet with some believers who had only received John's baptism. He preaches in the synagogue for three months and then moves over to the hall of Tyrannus where he continues preaching daily for the next two and a half years. During this time Epaphras and others evangelized other cities in the area such as Colossae, Hierapolis, etc. — Acts 19:1-41; I Cor. 15:32; 16:8-9; Col. 1:7; 4:12

THE THIRD MISSIONARY JOURNEY: I CORINTHIANS

- Paul apparently makes a second trip to Corinth, where he is humbled by their lack of repentance, etc. Sometime after this, members of Chloe's house church in Cenchrea arrive and tell Paul about problems in the Corinthian church; i.e. divisions, immorality, people rising up against Paul, etc. Soon after, a delegation arrives asking questions to certain doctrinal issues. Paul writes I Corinthians in response to all of this. Sometime after this, he writes a hard letter to them, confronting them. He sends the letter with Titus. After this, Paul has the incident with Demetrius and the other idol makers. — II Cor. 12:14; 13:1-2; I Cor. 1 & 2; 7:1; II Cor. 12:21; II Cor. 2:1-4

57
THE THIRD MISSIONARY JOURNEY: II CORINTHIANS

57
- Paul leaves Ephesus and travels to Troas, where he stays some time waiting for Titus to arrive with word from Corinth. When he doesn't arrive, Paul goes on to Philippi. — Acts 20:1; II Cor. 2:12-13; 7:5-8
- While in Philippi, Titus shows up with the good news that most of the church in Corinth had repented. Paul writes II Corinthians. Another thing occurring during all of this is Paul's desire to — II Cor. 7:9-16; 13:1-10

take up an offering for the poor of Jerusalem. He passes through Macedonia collecting money from the church toward this offering.

I Cor. 16:1-9

- Also during this time he apparently travels north all the way up into or close to the area of Illyricum.

Romans 15:19-21
Acts 20:2-3

- Finally, having sent II Corinthians, he personally sets out for Corinth.

THE THIRD MISSIONARY JOURNEY: ROMANS & GALATIANS

- While in Corinth, he writes the epistles to the Romans and probably Galatians, also.

Rom. 16

TRIP TO JERUSALEM & ARREST

58 • Paul, now in the company of ambassadors from several cities; travels by land back up to Macedonia, picking up Luke in Philippi, and then on to Troas, where he stays with the brethren for a week. The young man falls from the window but Paul brings him back to life.

Acts 20:4-12

- The party then travels on to Miletus, where Paul spends some time with the Ephesian elders.

I Cor. 16:2 (Sabbath)
Acts 20:13-38

- The party then sails for Caesarea, after a brief stop in Acre (Ptolimais).

Acts 21:1-14

- In Caesarea, they stay at the house of Philip the evangelist and Paul is warned again about Jerusalem.

- They then travel to Jerusalem, where they meet with the elders and Paul agrees to take part in a Jewish vow.

Acts 21:15-26

- While in the temple praying, a mob rushes upon Paul and tries to kill him but he is rescued by the Romans. He gives a speech to them but they become all the angrier.

Acts 21:27-22:29

- The Romans take him to the Sanhedrin where there is a great uproar over his beliefs in resurrection.

Acts 22:30-23:10

- Paul is visited by the Lord who reassures him. He is sent to Caesarea at night because of the Jewish plot to kill him.

Acts 23:11-35

- While there he appears before Felix.

Acts 24:1-26

58-60 • Paul remains in custody in Caesarea for two years.

THE TRIP TO ROME

- Festus replaces Felix and tries to convince Paul to appear in Jerusalem. Paul appeals to Caesar.

Acts 24:27

- Festus consults with Agrippa (II) who hears Paul's testimony.

Acts 25:1-26:29

60 • Festus sends Paul to Rome.

Acts 25:21; 26:30-32

- Paul sails for Rome, suffers shipwreck on the way.

Acts 27:1-28:14

61-63 • Paul spends two years in Rome in rented quarters.

Acts 28:15-31

ROME: PHILEMON, COLOSSIANS AND EPHESIANS

- Paul writes Philemon, Colossians and Ephesians.

ROME: PHILIPPIANS

- Paul writes Philippians.

PAUL'S ACQUITTAL AND TRAVELS: I TIMOTHY AND TITUS

63 • He is acquitted and then travels to Ephesus, where he leaves Timothy. He travels to Macedonia
64 where he writes I Timothy. He also travels to Crete, where he leaves Titus, then to Miletus where
64-68 he leaves Trophimus (sick), on to Spain (according to early writers) and Nicopolis, where he writes Titus.

I Timothy 1:3; Titus 1:5;
II Tim. 4:20; Titus 3:12

PAUL'S ARREST AND DEATH: II TIMOTHY

68

- He eventually makes it to Troas where it is likely he is suddenly arrested and sent to Rome.

II Timthy 4:13

- In Rome he writes II Timothy and soon after is beheaded.

II Timothy 4:6-8, 18

NOTES

INTRODUCTION
1. D. Martyn Lloyd-Jones, *An Exposition of Ephesians*, Vol. 1 (Grand Rapids, MI: Baker Books, 1978) p. 367.

WEEK 2
1. Steve Gallagher, *At the Altar of Sexual Idolatry* (Dry Ridge, KY: Pure Life Ministries, 2000) p. 260-261.
2. D. Martyn Lloyd-Jones, *God's Way of Reconciliation* (Grand Rapids, MI: Baker Books, 1972) p. 77, 79.
3. *ibid.,* p. 108-113.

WEEK 3
1. A. W. Tozer, *God Tells the Man Who Cares* (Camp Hill, PA: Christian Publications,1992).
2. D. Martyn Lloyd-Jones, *The Unsearchable Riches of Christ* (Grand Rapids, MI: Baker Books, 1998) p. 5-6.

WEEK 4
1. *Pulpit Commentary, Ephesians 4*, as cited in *AGES Digital Library* (Rio, WI: AGES Software, Inc., 2001) p. 20-21.
2. Steve Gallagher, "The Searing of the Conscience," *Unchained webzine*, archived at purelifeministries.org.
3. W. J. Conybeare and J. S. Howson, *The Life and Epistles of St. Paul*, (Grand Rapids, MI: Wm. B. Eerdman's Publishing Co., 1978) p. 165-166.

WEEK 5
1. Albert Barnes, *Notes on the Bible*, as cited in *AGES Digital Library* (Rio, WI: AGES Software, Inc., 2000) p. 202.
2. Steve Gallagher, *Living In Victory*, (Dry Ridge, KY: Pure Life Ministries, 2002) p. 181, 188-189, 190-191.

WEEK 6
1. Steve Gallagher, *Intoxicated with Babylon*, (Dry Ridge, KY: Pure Life Ministries, 2001) p. 59-60.
2. A. W. Tozer, *The Best of A. W. Tozer*, compiled by Warren Wiersbe (Grand Rapids, MI: Baker Book House, 1978) p. 76, 186.
3. Gallagher, *Intoxicated with Babylon*, p. 193-194.

WEEK 7
1. Steve Gallagher, *Irresistible to God*, (Dry Ridge, KY: Pure Life Ministries, 2003) p. 129-130.
2. *ibid.*, 108-109.
3. A. T. Robertson, *Robertson's Word Pictures*, as cited in *e-Sword*, accessed at www.e-Sword.net.
4. Young-Hoon Lee, as quoted by Glenn Meldrum, *Rend the Heavens*, (Scottsdale, AZ: In His Presence Ministries, 2004) p. 154.

WEEK 8
1. Gallagher, *Intoxicated with Babylon*, p. 66-67, 70.

WEEK 9

1. *Pulpit Commentary, Jeremiah 32*, as cited in *AGES Digital Library* (Rio, WI: AGES Software, Inc., 2001) p. 14.
2. Conybeare and Howson, p. 178-179.

WEEK 10

1. Alexander MacLaren, *Expositor's Bible: Colossians*, as cited in *AGES Digital Library* (Rio, WI: AGES Software, Inc., 2002) p. 46.
2. Martin Luther, *Preface to the Epistle to the Romans: Part II*, as cited in *AGES Digital Library* (Rio, WI: AGES Software, Inc., 2000) p. 17.

WEEK 11

1. Ed Bulkley, *Why Christians Can't Trust Psychology*, (Eugene, OR: Harvest House Publishers, 1993) p. 325-326.
2. MacLaren, p. 147-148.
3. Barnes, p. 413.
4. Conybeare and Howson, p. 612.

WEEK 12

1. Matthew Henry, *Matthew Henry's Commentary on the Whole Bible: Colossians*, accessed at www.ccel.org.
2. Gallagher, *Living in Victory*, p. 72-73.
3. Barnes, p. 873.
4. Philip Schaff, *History of the Christian Church*, Vol. 1, as cited in *AGES Digital Library* (Rio, WI: AGES Software, Inc., 2000) p. 308-309.

THE WALK OF REPENTANCE

A 24-WEEK GUIDE TO PERSONAL TRANSFORMATION

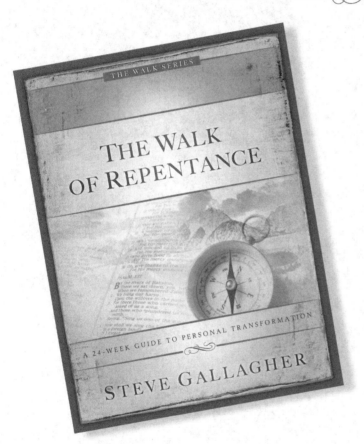

EXPERIENCE THE TIMES OF REFRESHING THAT FOLLOW REPENTANCE

The one thing believers in America don't need more of is information about Christianity. We know more about it than any people who have ever lived. Our problem isn't a lack of knowledge. Our problem is a lack of living it.

This 24-week Bible study has impacted the lives of thousands of people because it equips them to live out the Word of God. It is a simple, straightforward discipleship tool that focuses on the basics of the Christian life. Each week of this easy-to-use curriculum has a theme, addressing the challenges of the Christian life one step at a time.

Whether used by individuals, small groups or couples, in counseling settings, Sunday school classes or prison ministry, *The Walk of Repentance* makes a profound impact and leads sensitive hearts into a deeper intimacy with the Lord.

A LAMP UNTO MY FEET

A 12-WEEK STUDY THROUGH PSALM 119

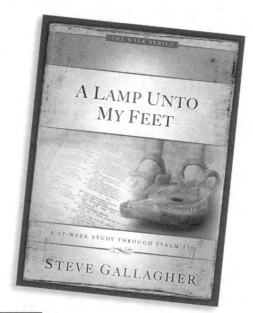

EVERY READER WILL BE BROUGHT INTO A DEEPER LOVE, RESPECT AND APPRECIATION FOR GOD'S WORD.

A Lamp Unto My Feet, a sequel to *The Walk of Repentance*, is a 12-week journey through the beautiful Psalm 119. This practical, personal study is a great resource for any individual seeking guidance in the midst of life's struggles. Through daily meditation readings and questions for reflection, believers will be asked to consider the truths of Scripture. At each week's end they will also read about the life of David, a man after God's own heart and author of this epic psalm. Every reader will be brought into a deeper love, respect and appreciation for God's Word.

HE LEADS ME BESIDE STILL WATERS

A 12-WEEK STUDY THROUGH THE CHOICEST PSALMS

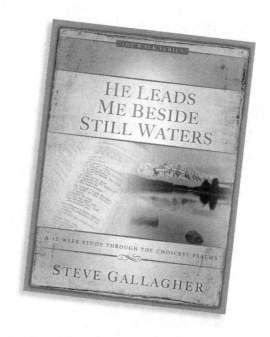

A PRACTICAL STUDY FOR THE HEART THAT SEEKS TO KNOW AND WORSHIP GOD.

"The Book of Praises," as ancient worshipers of Jehovah called the Psalms, is a fitting name for a book in which the adoration of God is the prominent theme. God's glorious attributes are revealed in a variety of ways: His sovereignty, majesty, power, mercy, compassion and trustworthiness are all poetically illuminated for us in the Psalms. Every word penned emits the aroma of humble worship and reverential fear.

In the Psalms, we have been bequeathed a treasury of the most profound interactions between pious men and a loving, caring God. This 12-week study of the choicest Psalms takes you right into those intimate exchanges and evokes a determined desire to find His Presence for yourself.